How to Become a
Successful Consultant
in Your Own Field

About the Author

Hubert Bermont received his education at New York University undergraduate and graduate schools. He has written eighteen books—eight of them on the subject of consulting—and is a frequent lecturer on consulting at colleges and universities.

Mr. Bermont, formerly the Editor-in-Chief of The Consultant's Library, is a senior member of the faculty at The Consultants Institute. He is the nation's foremost consultant's consultant—teaching, advising, coaching, and inspiring independent consultants in every field; his counsel has been considered the most important factor in their success.

HOW TO ORDER

Quantity discounts are available from the publisher, Prima Publishing & Communications, P.O. Box 1260BER, Rocklin, CA 95677; telephone (916) 624-5718. On your letterhead include information concerning the intended use of the books and the number of books you wish to purchase.

U.S. Bookstores and Libraries: Please submit all orders to St. Martin's Press, 175 Fifth Avenue, New York, NY 10010; telephone (212) 674-5151.

How to Become a Successful Consultant in Your Own Field

Revised, Updated
Expanded edition

Hubert Bermont

Prima Publishing & Communications
P.O. Box 1260BER
Rocklin, CA 95677
(916) 624-5718

Typography by Miller Freeman Publications
Production by Bookman Productions
Jacket design by The Dunlavey Studio

Prima Publishing & Communications
Rocklin, CA

Library of Congress Cataloging-in-Publication Data

Bermont, Hubert Ingram.
How to become a successful consultant in your own field.

Includes index.
1. Business consultants.   I.   Title.
HD69.C6B47   1989   658.4′6   88-32384
ISBN 0-914629-90-5

89   90   91   92   RRD   10   9   8   7   6   5   4   3

Printed in the United States of America

Preface

The first edition of this book was originally written and published in 1978. To my delight and surprise, it went through eight printings and sold over fifty thousand copies. But it did several other important things as well.

The book became the cornerstone and foundation for the eventual Consultant's Library, the largest international publisher to the consulting profession. It also surprisingly made me the nation's leading consultant's consultant. As such, I have since had several hundred consultants discussing their problems in my office and seeking assistance in setting up their own consultancies in their own fields. Further, I have been asked to conduct seminars and workshops on the subject of consulting. Here I learned a lot about what other consultants are doing—where they are failing and where they are succeeding.

The result of all this activity has been to gain knowledge which far exceeds the contents of the original book. The basic information in the first edition has not been changed due to the many thousands of letters I received from readers telling me how closely they identified with my odyssey. But the tricks of the trade which I have since learned and the changing society we live in have made it imperative that the book be both updated and enlarged to its present state.

I am indebted to my wife Kimberlee for urging and inspiring me to write this second edition.

Hubert Bermont

Contents

Introduction

Much has been written about the "middle-age crisis," about male and female menopausal depression, about the thrashing around that comes at a certain time of life when one asks one's self "What's it all about?" Doctors of every stripe have theories, TV panelists devote endless hours discussing causes and remedies, while the other media join the cacophony.

True, there are biological and hormonal changes occurring at that time of life, and they are somewhat akin to adolescence. But this parallel is overworked *ad nauseum*—to the point that the individual in question is most often stripped of whatever maturity he or she has gained after weathering half a lifetime. However, the primary difference between the middle-aged person and the adolescent is never discussed in this context, that is the anxious, frightened anticipation of the young adult in projecting his future versus the depression of the matured person in reflecting on his past. Whence comes this depression (setting aside any hormonal changes, which may or may not occur)? The "experts" don't deal with this.

The depression comes from looking back and discovering that in your line of work or in your profession you may not have been the cause of your own experience. Wherever you are in the table of organization, there is someone or some board taking full charge of your actions or decisions, withholding full credit or compensation for those things you have done expertly, and overcharging you for your errors. This authority makes the rules, breaks the rules, and changes the rules—sometimes in mid-project. This authority sets standards at will. This authority delegates responsibility, withholds responsibility, and accepts responsibility at its own convenience. But most of all, this authority offers you and your family a living or takes it away at will—and therein lies the ultimate power. The threat and the promise, implied or stated. The situation is endemic to the table of organization itself.

How is it possible, then, for a person to be a part of this rat race for an extended period of time without looking back and feeling anxiety and depression, without feeling unfulfilled and trapped? It isn't possible. To wave it away by typing it or labelling it"middle-age crisis" or some other euphemism is to demean the individual who wants more out of his or her life's work and who wants a sense of self actualization. This book is based on the fact that his fulfillment will never be forthcoming from a "superior" any more than it is ever forthcoming from a parent or any other authority figure. To expect it is to be trapped in your own childhood.

There are other books which deal with "the executive drop-out," with "alternative lifestyles," etc. This is not one of them. I address myself to the individual who has gained a goodly amount of expertise and experience in a given field, who has been aware for some time of being trapped in an uncomfortable working situation, who realizes that changing employers will only be more of the same because the house rules are stacked against him by the very nature of the system, and who has at least once thought "Maybe I ought to try consulting."

I wish I could say that I was one of those organizational drop-outs who one day decided that the rat race was even harmful to rats and that my superiors and the corporation could all go to hell. However, such was not the case; heroism has never played any part in my kharma. In truth, after having worked for ten years in an executive capacity for a company (from the age of thirty-three to the age of forty-three), after having brought that part of the company which was my responsibility from $1,100,000 to $2,600,000 in sales, and after having refused a promotion within the company which would have meant relocating to a city I detest, the authority called me in one day and fired me. The exact words were: "You are going nowhere with the company and the company is going nowhere with you." Although that was the most important positive event in my entire working career (in hindsight), I went into total shock at the time. They really did me a favor, but they will get no credit for it here, since they did not have my interests at heart. Indeed, I had done such a good job at training my assistant that they were able to replace me with him at less than two-thirds my salary.

Up to this point, I, too, had been suffering nagging depression, anxiety, and general malaise. My work, for a couple of years, simply wasn't gratifying. But I chalked it up to some kind of middle-age thing, having read everything on the subject. I had found myself, in part or in whole, in every case history I studied.

How I handled this trauma in the next few weeks and the course I embarked upon will be revealed in a subsequent chapter of this book. The point is that it isn't necessary to wait until "they" do anything if you have any awareness of your own suffering. They do it *to* you; you can do it *for* yourself.

The unknown always produces fear. The profession of consulting is fairly unknown and uncharted. One of the reasons for this is that it is part of the consultant's stock in trade to wrap himself in a cloak of sagacity and mystique. The other reason is that there is no college degree which leads to a consultancy (with the singular exception of The Consultant's Institute which offers certification—C.P.C.—via excellent home study courses). The purpose of this book is to offer a basic primer in becoming a consultant. To do this we shall look behind the curtain, so to speak, and strip away the mystique.

Chapter One

Who Is a Consultant?

Some years ago, I spotted a familiar face at the airport. No mistake about it, it was Ben. A wave of nostalgia came over me. We had been college friends thirty years back. The head was bald and the girth increased, but the mischievous, pixie face was the same. Lots of bear-hugs and reminiscences of capers on campus. Ben had been a renegade and an upstart. A brilliant boy, he'd had the grudging respect of his fellow students and his teachers. But he was always in some kind of trouble. Then the conversation came around to "So what are you up to these days?" Ben is president of his own successful consulting firm. How did it happen? "I got tired of being fired," he said in a straightforward manner.

Ben isn't typical. There is no typical consultant. But he has certain traits that are requisite for a successful career in consulting, albeit these traits alone do not guarantee success. At school, he had a quick, receptive, and retentive mind. He questioned everything—a bane to his instructors. He would not and could not abide "chickenshit." He ignored red-tape. Socially accepted custom was anathema to him unless he could see some private or public good in it. He dropped out or was kicked out of a num-

1

ber of courses; but those in which he was interested and to which he applied himself, he was straight "A." Ben never seemed to care what others thought of him—neither his peers nor his betters. But he did appear to be grading himself all the time according to his own standards. Most of all, he loved a good laugh. To him, the world was an amusing spectacle. He was able to maintain this attitude throughout the war, but never ignored its tragedy. Some called this courage, others called it fearlessness; I call it a spirit of adventure. Ben has been married more than once. When things weren't right for him, he either tried to fix them or moved on. He has never stayed for very long in a bad or uncomfortable situation. He has never found himself permanently trapped.

This vignette fairly well sums it up. If you are indecisive, dour, fatalistic, deterministic, plodding, or pessimistic, stick to what you are doing and don't consider a consulting career for yourself. These qualities are listed without pejoration. If everyone became a consultant, our whole society would fall apart. As Lao Tze put it, "If every sentient being in this world was a bumblebee, there would be no bumblebees." A consultant is like a lawyer; he is also like a psychiatrist. (These two comparisons will be used frequently throughout the book.) Both must, first and foremost, be good listeners. But like common sense, that quality is not too common. Listening is an art. Ask any lawyer how much money his average client wastes by thrashing around emotionally hour after hour in his office until the facts in the case present themselves clearly so that the lawyer may act intelligently. Ask any psychiatrist how often a patient comes to him with a problem which is not the problem at all but merely a smokescreen for the real one, almost always. Since you don't know what the problem is, you must have the gift of listening intently with both ears plus Theodore Reik's "third ear." You must be receptive.

I have often heard it said that a consultant primarily must be an objective person. Not necessarily. He might be an opinionated lout. Objectivity in the human animal is automatic when he is not emotionally involved in a problem or situation. What is required here is technique, not objectivity as a personal trait. Child psychiatrists can be of enormous help to other people's children because of the techniques they use, even though these same techniques are unworkable on some of their own unmanageable children because of the emotional involvement. A fine surgeon will rarely operate on a close friend or relative. Emotional involvement cancels out objectivity; lack of it guarantees it. Your strength as a consultant lies primarily in your ability to listen receptively. Only in this way can you identify the real problem as opposed to what the client ofttimes thinks it is, and then get to work solving it.

You must question everything. Only a curious person can do this and do it effectively. The more information you have, the better you can work. If you are not curious by nature don't try consulting as a career, because you will fail.

Adventurousness almost to the point of heresy is another important quality. One of the reasons a client is in trouble is that he has been doing the same things with the same attitudes for too long without self-examination. It is possible for you to be brash without being disrespectful. The really big assignments come often to those who are able to run the fine line in this area. Here is a verbatim conversation with a prospective client, the president of a growing conglomerate:

He: I want you to help me build an empire here.
Me: Fair enough. You want to be an emperor.
He: I didn't say that.
Me: Yes you did. I'm not judging you. You want to

be an emperor. Let's get to work and see how
we can accomplish this.

He: I've never had any employee talk to me this
way before.

Me: Maybe that's one of your troubles. Besides,
I'm not your employee. I'm a consultant, who,
for a fee, would like to help you actualize your
goals.

That cemented the relationship in that instance. I earned
$5100 in fees and was of considerable help to him. Of
course, you can't take this approach, or any other, with
everyone. You have to be able to size up whom you are
dealing with. But this in itself is an adventure. It is off-
beat. It's fun. You must be able to enjoy each encounter.
I have never met a successful humorless consultant.

You must be a person with extremely high standards
for yourself—and be self-motivated enough to constantly push yourself to meet those standards. In other words,
an inner-directed person makes a good consultant. If you
are still trying to please "the boss" (your client) you will
surely fail. The client has been self-indulgent for too
long and his employees have been yessing him to death.
That is why he is in trouble and has called upon you. If
he can coerce or browbeat you into doing what he wants,
he has no use for you in the first place, and, even though
you may come away with a fee, you will lose your self-
confidence. Remember, your self-confidence is one of
your main tickets to success.

There are all kinds of books and courses these days
that deal with something called "assertiveness training."
If you feel you need this kind of training, forget consulting. Put another way, the consulting experience implies
assertiveness. Look at the situation itself. The prospective client called you; you didn't call him. He is in trouble; you are not. He has money or "face" to lose; you do

not. All of this ensures your ability to come on strong. We are assuming, of course, that you are an expert in your field, because, above all, you must be right. Your strength in this situation builds the client's confidence in you. Consider the physician who displays a lack of assurance in his own diagnosis. The patient loses respect. The patient lacks confidence in the proposed cure. The patient does not cooperate. The patient does not recuperate too quickly. The doctor's reputation suffers. The patient does not recommend others. The doctor cannot raise his fees. A client's initial confidence resulting from the consultant's self-assuredness means that there is already a 75 percent chance that the project will be successful due to mutual cooperation.

Never forget that, at the very least, you are in a peer situation. If you can't shake the old attitude that a person in a high position (usually the one who is considering retaining your services) is your superior, you are in trouble.

These, then, are the characteristics of a potentially successful consultant. But what do you have to know?

Chapter Two

Expertise

"**M**ost of us who have been involved in any industry or profession for a long time, don't know what we know." This wisdom was given to me by a very smart friend and client, a lady who is president of her own small successful corporation. It's true. Invariably, when we come to assess our own accumulated knowledge, we come up short. Not because we necessarily think little of ourselves. It is just that we have no full cognizance at that moment of the vast wealth of information we have picked up and stored along the way. But if we are jogged, usually in the form of questions put to us as consultants, we seem to experience almost total recall in areas in which we thought ourselves ignorant. It's almost as though we become mnemonists. This is because we are thinking professionally—for money; and our powers of concentration are enormous in this milieu.

Several years ago, I received a phone call from a magazine writer requesting an interview. She was preparing an article concerning a segment of my industry that I had never dealt with directly. I told her so. She pressed for the interview anyhow. Arriving with her tape recorder the following week, she put only two questions to me. To my amazement, I taped an hour and fifteen minutes of continuous information. I had obviously learned a great deal over the years in the interface of that part of the industry with my own.

In my second year of consulting, I was already earning more than I had at any previous point in my entire working life, and I was enjoying my new free life to the fullest. One day, I caught myself thinking, "What a fool I was to have sweated and toiled all those years for the honor and glory of a thankless corporation. I should have been doing this right from the beginning. This is the life." But I quickly realized the nonsense and lack of logic in this kind of thinking. Without the experience and contacts I had gained, and without the reputation I had acquired in my field as a result of that experience and those contacts, I could never have become a consultant in the first place. In mid-life, if you really sit down to contemplate it, you come to the realization that your entire working life is the sum total of cause/effect relationships that led you to where you are now.

How many years of experience are necessary? That is difficult to pin down. It depends upon many variables: the field itself, your position in that field, how well known you are, whether or not you have been published in book form or trade magazine articles, your age. But certainly no less than five years and no more than fifteen. Tevya sings in *Fiddler on the Roof* "When you're rich, they think you really know." For our purposes, we could paraphrase by saying "When you're older, they think you really know." Indeed, consulting is one of the few professions wherein older age is a help rather than a hindrance, because most people believe that wisdom comes only with years of experience—even though "it ain't necessarily so." I had a cousin who was a student at a dental college. The entire family urged him on to successful graduation by promising to become his patients on the very day that he would open his first office. Came the day, and no one showed up. When he questioned them, they invariably answered "Maybe when you're a little longer in the line, Sonny." You may feel that you know enough to become a consultant at a very early age. But, unless you have already racked up an impressive and renowned set of credentials, you are bound to be thwarted by "What does that young whippersnapper think he can show me?" Next, it is incumbent upon you to make a realistic evaluation of the marketability of your expertise, experience, and knowledge. Is it saleable in your industry? To whom? Is it needed? Will you be performing a legitimate function in your field? A "hype" may get you by for a year or two (if you are clever) but be assured that at the end of that time you will be pounding the pavements looking for a job again—with a tremendous loss of self-esteem and "face." Sit down with a pencil and paper and inventory your skills and your experience. Go back over your previous jobs. Go all the way back to your first job, and even before that to your part-time jobs at school. Everything was a learning experience. And this will be the first time that you will be able to synergistically use all of this learning. You won't believe the kinds of information your clients will need from you. On the other hand, perhaps you will believe it further on in the book. Everything you have ever done, read, seen, and studied will come into play in consulting work.

In my own case, having come out of the shock of being peremptorily fired, I went home to think about my ten years with the company. During that time—and because I had spent so much time in the same place and performed the same functions—many people had come to me for advice. These were people outside of my company. They asked everything from highly technical questions to how to start a similar but smaller business. I gave the advice freely, because I have always liked people. I gave it freely in the other sense, because to charge for my advice would have constituted a conflict of interests. Obviously, there was a market for this kind of service. I decided to give it a go. I really had no alternative, since I knew that I would never take on a regular "job" again for the rest of my life. No one would fire me ever again.

All I had to do was surmount the supreme hurdle. I had to get started.

Chapter Three

Getting Started

At the outset, I must confess that the worst and most precarious, if not dangerous, way to get started is by getting fired from your previous position. Ben and I made it, but I'm certain that there were outside forces (such as timing and luck), which had nothing to do with our talents, that played an important role in it all coming together. In my own case, I was desperate—financially and otherwise; I simply had to make it happen. As Mel Brooks, the comic who plays the two-thousand-year-old man, put it when asked the primary means of locomotion in his primitive days in the jungle with wild beasts, "Fear. Fear was the main source of propulsion." First, whether your dismissal was for good cause or not, it will be on the industrial grapevine in no time and will hurt your reputation. Second, this situation does not give you enough financial leeway and time to plan your new profession carefully.

But the main reason for quitting your job to become a consultant while you are still in the company's good graces is that it gives you an excellent chance to leave with a flying start: your current employer could well be your first client. This almost always guarantees a successful career, financially and otherwise. It also makes all

11

kinds of sense for you and your employer. He has a need for you or you wouldn't be working there today. Just show him that you can perform the same services as competently (if not more so) at approximately one-third to one-half your current salary, pointing out all the while that he needn't continue to pay any more benefits, retirement, social security, or taxes in your behalf, and you should be retained—unless, of course he is an utter fool or some arbitrary nonsensical corporate policy forbids this, in which case you should have quit a long time ago anyway.

As an independent, no longer confined to restricted working hours, working days, and a working place, no longer required to attend endless meetings, some of which have nothing to do with your particular work and responsibilities, and no longer restricted to dealing laterally with other employees, you can accomplish more for the company than you do now in less than one-third the time—and that time is of your choosing. This is not theory; it is established fact. House counsels have established their own law practices this way, directors of advertising have started their own agencies this way, accountants have set up their own offices this way, engineers have started their own consulting firms this way—the list is endless.

The major accomplishment here is two-fold. First, it gives you a financial base or "floor" at the outset. That initial retainer will pay for all of your start-up costs: office rent, telephone, postage, insurance, stationery, and some "walking-around" money to get more clients. Second, and equally important, the additional clients will come in faster knowing that they are not mere guinea pigs in some personal experiment of yours to start a new thing for yourself at their expense. They will think, and rightly so, that if you were able to resign your former position and your company still thought highly enough of you to buy your expertise, you must be good enough for them. In short, you're virtually home free.

If you can't pull this off and you are either fired or just quit, you are in the same boat that I was in on that fateful day years ago. No cash in the bank, a severance check for $2400, an apartment, a son, and a car to support—and no prospects. I narrate my actions at that time as accurately as possible with the fond hope that the reader will learn some things from my successes and failures and apply them to his or her own situation.

Having cleared out my things from my previous office, I went over them very carefully at home. I quickly realized that my desk telephone and address book was the most important item in my possession as far as my new plan was concerned. Ten years of business contacts were clearly recorded and up-to-date. I wasted no time. For the next three days I telephoned everyone and anyone to personally let them know what I was doing and why they could no longer reach me at my old number. Never trust your former employer, switchboard operator or successor to tell the world your whereabouts. Also, "Mr. _____ is no longer with us" gives the caller the eerie feeling that he is calling the undertaker. I must have made over a hundred phone calls with no specific purpose in mind except to let people know that I was no longer with the firm. It was then I learned the truth of the old adage "Throw enough seeds on the ground and something is bound to grow." One friend, who operated a two-person office in a totally different field, told me that he had just landed a big contract that required that he be out of the city two-thirds of the time. He was reluctant to leave his office in the charge of his brand new secretary. In view of my excellent previous record in training executive secretaries in my former company, would I consider training his? In return, I could use his office as my own at only one-third the rent (it was a very prestigious building), I could have free unlimited use of the secretary and free use of the telephone; I was, of course, to pay for my own long-distance calls.

I readily accepted and gave the nearest printer a rush order for stationery and cards bearing my new address, my new telephone number, and my new self-awarded title.

I then placed a news item in my trade journal stating that I was now on my own, giving the phone number where I could be reached. That brought nothing but a few good wishes.

At this juncture, the worst parallel between a consultant and a doctor comes into focus. Like physicians, consultants generally don't advertise their services. It isn't against the law or anything; it's just that advertising doesn't work effectively in consulting. So I sat in my new office with my new stationery, my new telephone number, my new calling cards, and even new billheads—and it dawned on me that nobody was going to call me because nobody knew I was there. I studied those calling cards and realized why they had that nomenclature. I would have to call on people and leave them.

I made three telephone calls to former colleagues. In each case, when I was asked why I wanted an appointment (either by the executive himself or by his secretary), I honestly said that I was seeking consulting work. All three immediately put me off with some ridiculous excuse or other. I thought about that for a while. I tried three others, but with a different approach. This time I utilized my previously hard-won reputation. When asked the inevitable question, I came on as a peer and said that I merely wanted to kick around a few old and new concepts regarding our industry. All three agreed to appointments, albeit one made it three weeks hence. I was careful not to invite them to lunch for fear that they might feel obligated to return a favor. I was right on target there. I learned that what must be overcome in these calls is any feeling on the part of the recipient that you are looking for a favor or a job. Remember, nine chances out of ten, he knows that you have lost your job or quit without getting another one. He automatically assumes that all is not well with you. If you have ever done him a favor in your past dealings with him in your former position, that is even worse. In that first contact, he must be made to understand that things are fine with you and that you have finally found your place in the world—as indeed you have. He will then relax.

Having then set up half a dozen meetings in this fashion, I firmly resolved not to allow the discussions to consist of idle, time-wasting chatter. I was also careful to remind myself that these were peer-level meetings, not interviews. I set to meticulously doing my homework. In each instance, I plotted the recent history of the company as well as that of the executive in question. I laid out several topics for discussion, all leading to what I surmised to be the company's problems at the time. This was the easiest part. Every company has problems. I projected the mundane solutions they had probably come up with and even possibly tried. The clincher was to be several new approaches of my own. If this sounds mystical or crystal-ballish, it isn't. As we shall discuss later and in greater detail, virtually all organizations within a given field suffer pretty much the same problems. My own previous employer was no exception, so I had spent a good deal of time and effort wrestling with those very same problems; I had also listened attentively to my friends with other companies when they complained about the state of the industry.

If I haven't come right out and said this before, I certainly meant to imply it, even though it sounds snotty: every consultant worth his salt thinks he is just one degree smarter than anyone else. That's how you dare look

the man in the eye and describe some innovative solutions to his problems. At any rate, I made quite an im-
pression and assumed that I was doing fine.

So what happened as a result of all that brilliant talk
in those memorable, hard-earned meetings? Did I have
them eating out of my hand and did I walk away with six
new clients? Not on your tintype. I struck out every time.
The fatal question was "For whom are you doing consulting work now? Which companies have retained you
thus far?" No point in lying; they would have checked it
out. My truthful answer was received like a case of lepro-
sy. "No one yet. I'm only now getting started. You will
be the first." Even if I had foreseen this (which I hadn't
in my cockeyed euphoria over my new life), there would
have been no way around it. Nobody wants to be the first
to do anything, except possibly to walk on the moon.
Now I recalled my cousin, the new dentist. Now I recalled the number of people who tried to start new publications or launch any new kind of product. All to no
avail. I would not be defeated. The situation required a
lot of pondering, and ponder I did—for two weeks. This
produced only one conclusion. Whatever I did had to be
daring, different, and unorthodox. I decided to steal a
page from the life of Mark Twain, a man I had come to
love and admire through all of his writings.

After unsuccessfully trying to mine silver in the de-
sert with his brother, Mark Twain arrived in San Francis-
co penniless. He went to the most illustrious newspaper
and applied for a job as a reporter. He was told that there
were no jobs available because there was no budget to
pay for additional personnel. He told them that he required no compensation, that he only wanted to write for
them. He was, of course, immediately accepted under
those terms (there were no labor union obstacles at that
time). Needless to say, his stories were published daily
and read with relish by the San Franciscans. A few weeks

later, Mr. Twain marched into his "employers" offices and resigned. They were horrified and angry. They took him to task for his unethical behavior. He reminded them that he was not being paid, a fact they had conveniently forgotten. He was immediately put on salary and given an assignment as foreign correspondent. I decided to do something similar.

The next time anyone asked me who had retained me, I would truthfully answer with the name of the finest, most prestigious and most successful name in the business. I quickly selected this firm, made an out-of-town phone call to their Mr. A., set up an appointment, and went to see him. I laid out an entire workload for myself and told him that I wanted to do this in my city for his company free of charge. I told him honestly what my motives were. He gladly accepted. Loaded with the materials he gave me, I didn't even wait until I got home, but went to work on the train; I couldn't afford the plane. It was necessary to force myself into a state of mind that dictated that I was indeed employed by that worthy company to run an office for them in my city and that I was to work for them as though I were being paid. I worked like hell in behalf of that firm, setting up meetings, solving problems, making projections, and filing daily progress reports. Within exactly two weeks, Mr. A. telephoned me, said he would be in my city the following week, and requested that I be his guest at lunch. It has been almost twenty years, but I vividly recall that when the food finally came, I was so relieved, so overjoyed, so grateful, and so proud that I couldn't eat a bite. Mr. A. had told me that they were not only impressed with my work but also overwhelmed by my approach, which, in turn, bespoke an innovative turn of mind. Well, Mark Twain takes the credit, but at the time I didn't mind giving myself a small pat on the back, too. Mr. A. then asked me what kind of retainer I wanted. I was in no position to consider what I was worth, how much his budget would allow, or how much his company would require of me. I quickly added up in my head my minimal office expense at the time, my apartment rent, food for myself and my son, and car payments and blurted out "One hundred dollars a week." "Done," he said, and we shook hands on it. No contract was signed. I was retained by that company continuously for the next six and a half years.

That was the door-opener for me. Let 'em ask who has retained me now, I thought. They did and I told them. If I was good enough for Mr. A., I was certainly good enough for them. And they agreed. Never mind all those kudos for Mr. Twain and myself. I owe an awful lot to Mr. A. He made it possible. I've told him often.

Chapter Four

Growing

Armed with my big credential in the form of my first big client, I repeated the initial process with twenty more phone calls to prior contacts. Again the discussion of industry problems with possible solutions. At the end of six months, I acquired two more clients at similar retainers. I was now earning almost as much as it had taken me twenty years to reach in my previous career. Only two out of twenty calls? You will find that this is an excellent percentage. Oh, it wasn't easy. There were innumerable meetings, broken appointments, dead-ends, follow-up phone calls, and even some rudeness. But it was early in the game for me. I had not yet learned the difference between a prospect, a suspect, and a deadbeat. I had also not learned that the world is full of people in responsible executive positions who spend endless hours in pointless conversation in their office just to kill time and keep themselves from really working.

The three projects I was working on concerned themselves with three different aspects of the industry. That made the work diversified and fun. I was enjoying it immensely. All three companies paid my monthly invoices promptly.

19

Then I studied my calling card again. There was that word in bold letters: CONSULTANT. But I wasn't consulting at all. I was working, in the same areas I had worked before. There appeared to be only one big difference. This time, I had three bosses, and they could all fire me at will. What had happened to my fantasy? Why wasn't I just sitting in my office, stroking my chin, and offering up wisdom by the hour like the Oracle of Delphi? Surely I hadn't made up this fantasy on my own. The mental image of such consultants must have come from somewhere. Certainly there are consultants in my own town who charge $100 and $200 an hour, who have large secretarial staffs in expensively decorated offices, whose appointment calendars are full, and who are being constantly sought after. Who are they?

The answer was simple, once I doped it out. They are ex-senators or others who have previously held high government positions at comparatively low salaries just waiting for the day when they could capitalize on their contacts without creating a conflict of interest. They are somewhat akin to the "five-percenters" of World War II fame, who made lots of money by introducing Businessman A to Government Agency Director B. Sometimes they are called influence peddlers. They are indeed people of influence—and that influence is for sale. Or it could be someone like a former director of the Internal Revenue Service, whose three-sentence advice could be worth a fortune to a large corporation seeking to legitimately find a new tax shelter. All of these people also have the word CONSULTANT emblazoned on their cards. But there the similarity stops. None of these people have any place in a book like this. Their prosperous careers are assured on the very day the news media announce their intentions. Their struggling days are over. They have no use for the precepts set forth in this book. They only need good management of their time and an excellent accountant and tax attorney. I taste of no sour grapes. I wish them all well. I wish I hadn't had to struggle to become a consultant. But I did. And so will you.

But back to my problem, if problem it was. It made no difference what I called myself, I wasn't a consultant in the true sense of the word. Nobody called upon me for advice. It's true, there was a need for me in the working area. That was gratifying because everyone has a need to be needed. I was earning a very decent living because of that need. It was time to analyze the situation based upon what I had learned thus far.

I attempted to discover some common elements in all thirty contacts I had made over the previous nine months. Here the only true talent I possess came to the fore. I am a musician with what is known as a "tin ear." I can "play back" almost verbatim every conversation I have ever had no matter when it occurred. Since I had not yet established myself as a sage, no one, obviously, was willing to pay me for the few hours it took me to assess their problems accurately and offer solutions. Also, whenever I offered a plan of action to attack a problem, I was regarded as some kind of nuisance whose only goal was to give that executive more work. In all the cases where I didn't score I met with a certain antagonism. Their posture was invariably "Look, our organization has been operating fairly well for a hundred years before you decided to become a consultant and come in here like a doctor to tell us we are sick. We cannot refute most of what you say, but we'll muddle through on our own, thank you." But this isn't what they really meant. I learned much later that the above was a complete euphemism for "I'm paid not to make waves. You are trying to make waves here. Even if I did try some of your suggestions, it would make me late for my five o'clock golf foursome, and that is out of the question. This organization is satisfied to have me sit here and decide not to make decisions. Get lost." But what about the exceptions? The ones who retained me? What did they have in common? Sad to say, another negative quality—which helped me considerably. There wasn't anything I was doing for those organizations that they couldn't have done for themselves—with the glaring exception of Mr. A's company, which was located in a different city. My work for them required an office in my town. They saved a considerable amount of money retaining me rather than opening a facility here or constantly commuting. In other cases, I may be downbeating the hands that fed me, but in a sense I'm downbeating myself as well. Two wrongs will have to make a right in this instance. I suppose one could give them the benefit of the doubt by allowing them the perspicacity of having costed out the work in advance and come up on the plus side by not paying me company benefits and other payroll items. But the inevitable conclusion was another big lesson in cynicism about the "working" world: Nobody Wants To Do His Own Laundry! Thus was born the free-lancer. Even free-lancers have other free-lancers doing their chores.

The term "free lance" is traced back to medieval times. A knight who was not bound into the personal service of any king, prince, or lord set his lance up for hire. He was, in short, a mercenary. He was free to fight for anyone, for a price. He owed no allegiance to anyone and could live his life as he chose. If he was expert, he did well. If he was not, he starved or was killed in a joust. If he didn't like the life in any particular fiefdom, he was free to move on.

That is the way I assessed my own situation at the time. Did I really have cause for discontent? No. True, any one of my bosses could fire me (as before), but he could not threaten me with my living, since it was highly improbable that all three would fire me at the same time. It is that threat that keeps most of the working world in a state of anxiety. The only other thing that could send me into starvation, like the knight of old, was being inept at my work. But I was good, and I knew it. I felt no anxiety. I was free—a free-lancer. The real consulting work was to come later, but I didn't know this at the time. I decided to stop fretting, to go out and get still more of this interesting and gratifying work, and to keep growing—and learning.

Chapter Five

The Life

Is the life of an independent professional or free-lancer as great as it is cracked up to be? Yes. Even greater. Once a basic living is obtained in anyone's career, it is really the lifestyle or quality of life, not the money, that produces the best rewards. The subject of money will be taken up in detail in the next two chapters. Here is a general description of what my life has been like in the last twenty years.

In spite of the accommodating arrangement with my friend, I left his office after four months and found one of my own. Sharing an office was too distracting for me. I discovered that office space in any city is a faddish thing. There is always one section of downtown that is very in and stylish. It is the area that affords the most "image." It is, naturally, the highest rent area. It has the most expensive restaurants, shops, and clubs. On the opposite end of the scale is the slum area of town. In between is the somewhat transient area from which most people are moving—either "up" or "down." This middle area has not yet acquired a bad reputation, because some very notable people and firms are still there. The buildings are well maintained. The neighborhood restaurants have good and moderately priced food. But, amazingly, the rents are not midway between the chic and the downtrodden areas. To be more specific, at that time, office space in a brand new building in the fashionable end of town cost $10 per square foot. The slum area cost $2 per square foot. I found an office in a very old, but very gracious building for $3 per square foot. For one hundred dollars a month I had a spacious, sunny, airy room measuring twenty feet by twenty feet. I had a real working wood-burning fireplace, free utilities, and free nightly char service. This was an elevator building in the heart of town. Because I was willing to sign a lease for more than a year, the landlord restored the woodwork, painted completely, and tore down a wall that had halved the space. He even allowed my dog to keep me company in the office.

I brought an old but serviceable typewriter from home, as well as a desk, a sofa, and two chairs. The library table, typewriter table, and desk chair I purchased from Goodwill Industries. I had the floor carpeted wall to wall, bought a new air conditioner, and installed a small refrigerator. My entire cash outlay was $659. I had and used all of the same equipment for ten years.

I splurged in only one area. I retained the best and most expensive answering service in the city. I knew that I would be keeping irregular office hours. Each and every phone call could have been of vital importance to me at that time, having made so many contacts and dropped so many calling cards. It was imperative that each call be answered promptly, efficiently, knowledgeably, and accurately.

A word here about answering services. They can be as good or as bad as you make them. In short order, the man or woman on your switchboard will know enough to answer as though he or she is indeed your personal secretary. But, just as in a regular office set-up, she will react according to how you, her boss, treat her. I have always made it a point to personally visit the service every six months so that the man or woman sees a face to go with the voice. He or she identifies more readily with my situation that way. If she errs or is neglectful, I always report this to the supervisor. This way she stays on her toes with the full realization that I don't accept laxity on my phone, especially at the premium prices they are charging. When she leaves that employ or is promoted, I repeat the process with the new person assigned to me. Of course, when your answerer goes to the wash room, is out sick, goes to lunch or on vacation, the situation is usually hopeless with the temporary replacement, and there is nothing you can do about it. By and large, I have found the telephone answering service to be of enormous assistance at a minimal cost. The next important thing I did was to have the signpainter write on the door below my name "By Appointment Only." This was of tremendous importance to me. First, it kept away most solicitors. Second, it informed anyone who might be upset by the office being closed and dark in the middle of the day, that this was the normal way of my doing business and that there was no cause for concern. Third, I was now free to come and go as I pleased without fear or worry that I might miss an important visit or phone call.

This freedom I keep talking about was (and is) extremely vital to me. It was the keystone of my new existence. It marked the difference between my old life and my new one. It is also something that most people don't handle too well after half a lifetime of structure and stricture. I took to it like a duck to water, as I always knew I would.

Not sharing the office with anyone gave me the freedom to act any way I pleased. It also gave me the luxury of solitude when I required it. Not having a secretary or paying a high rent gave me the financial freedom of turning away a few clients who were obnoxious. I never once felt that I was sacrificing "image" for this freedom. No one ever asked "What kind of a two-bit operation are you running there without a secretary?" Organizational clients always have me come to them; the meetings are always on their premises. Individual clients have always found my office peaceful, relaxing, charming, and conducive to good discussion. But most important, I like to work there.

Earlier in the book, I said that the average executive could accomplish many times the work in a fraction of the time, and do it better. The primary reason and condition for this is an atmosphere that allows for absolutely no interruptions. Total clarity of thought is a consultant's major asset. No one can think clearly if constantly interrupted. The average working person is besieged all day long with unexpected visitors, unexpected meetings, requests for immediate reports or action, salespeople, etc. Then there are the endless obtrusive phone calls. Imagine, if you can, shutting all of this off. Just like that! I did. In any two-hour uninterrupted period, I accomplish as much as I did formerly in an eight-hour day. And so can you. We all can. When I don't want phone calls, I simply don't pick up. The answering service has no way of knowing whether I'm in or not. A secretary in the office does know, and the caller can tell by her uneasiness when she has to lie about it.

For other reasons, at that time, I didn't need a secretary. I can hunt and peck accurately on a typewriter at thirty-five words per minute. As for bookkeeping, that required about fifteen minutes a week, once my accountant set it up. Certainly the sending of three invoices a month, the recording of those payments and the accurate detailing of my expenses didn't need another person. I was still in the initial stages. Later, I hired assistance, but that's further on in the story.

It is important that I work in an atmosphere that is most comfortable for me at the time. So, if I don't feel like being in the office, I work at home, and *vice versa*. All of my contacts are contained in a Wheeldex file; I keep a duplicate of this file at home. I have a telephone at home as well as a typewriter. Since my primary piece of equipment is my brain, I will, on beautiful sunny days, haul the equipment out to the park and work there. I work on planes, on trains, and in vacation resorts. I work in airports, the doctor's waiting room, and in reception areas of prospective clients. I have done some of the most creative thinking for my clients on long walks or behind the wheel on long, boring turnpikes.

I always work at my own pace, that is, when I please and as I please. When I embarked on a consulting career I was excitedly aware that my whole life would change. I knew that this life would be unorthodox, and I welcomed it. Like the song says, "Been down so long, it looked like up to me." Well, why do things by half measures? If I was no longer a rat in the rat race, why behave like I was still in the maze with the rest of the rats? Why work five days a week and take weekends off? Why work nine to five? Why go to the stores on Thursday nights and Saturdays with the crowds? Why take off on holidays? Why hit the road when everyone else does? Why get all my sleep at night? I certainly wouldn't be hurting anyone by answering the needs of my circadian rhythms. And I could accomplish much more, for myself and for my clients. That is what I did. My new set-up accommodated it very well.

If I can't sleep some nights because my brain won't turn off, I work then and there at home. I have a need to "get away" at least once a month for a few days. Usually this is taken care of by business trips. I have no need for complete leisure since the joy of my vocation has made it my avocation. If business doesn't take me away, I'll take off for a few days anyhow—anywhere. I avoid the waste of rush hours by keeping non-rush-hour schedules. I never have appointment conflicts; I don't have that many appointments.

Up to twenty years ago, I was an untravelled person. I simply couldn't afford it. Since then, my work has taken me to large cities and small towns from coast to coast as well as to Europe—all paid for by my clients.

This whole new life seemed idyllic to me at the beginning. Although I don't take it for granted now and still appreciate and enjoy every moment of it, it seems quite normal to me today. It appears very abnormal to those acquaintances in my town who see me come and go and who wonder what on earth I do for a living.

Chapter Six

The Fee

What to charge the client? A big and important question. Charge too much and you won't be working. Charge too little and the prospective client will look elsewhere thinking that you couldn't be very good nor your advice very worthwhile. So what's the right price?

When I started, the question had me stumped. I went for advice. I had supposed that the nearest thing to a consultant was a lawyer. So I visited a friend who was a senior partner in one of the most esteemed law firms in the city. More important, he was a man I respected. I asked him what he had charged when he'd first started out. He told me that this was the only subject not covered in his law school and that he had struggled with the problem for a long time. His "answer" was no help at all. He simply told me to honestly charge whatever I thought I was worth. Although I was aware that I was knowledgeable in my field and that I had been one of the most effective executives in my former company, I was now starting a new profession and attempting to do something I had never actually done before. At this point it would not have been unusual for anyone to feel somewhat worthless. I'd had experience in my field, but not as a consultant. There was no way around it, however. At some point, hopefully soon, some prospective client would ask "How much?" and I had to be prepared with an answer.

A story I had heard came to mind. Possibly it is apocryphal, but it surely was germane. It seems that a power plant broke down. Electrical service for a large geographical area was instantly cut, causing disaster. All sorts of engineering experts were called in, but to no avail. Finally, the top brass enlisted the services of a local old-timer who had worked at the plant many years back. He arrived with a hammer, went immediately to a particular spot in the enormous labyrinth of machinery, and tapped lightly on a pipe. The system started up again forthwith, and power was restored. Soon after, the man submitted his bill for $1,000.02. He had broken it down this way: $.02 for tapping the pipe; $1,000 for knowing where to tap.

As it happened, one year prior to my starting my new career, I had undergone a divorce. I went to a divorce lawyer who was acclaimed by most to be the best in town, having practiced divorce law exclusively for over forty years. I presented my case to him and asked his fee. I remember at the time I had $1100 in the bank—my total assets. He floored me with "Forty dollars an hour." Of course, lawyers can never tell you in advance how much time they will require to settle your case. I told him that I couldn't afford him, envisioning all the while some astronomical legal fee like three or four thousand dollars. He replied, "Look, I think you are being taken for a ride because of your ignorance of the law. I'll take the case because I have known you for a long time and because I like you. Furthermore, I believe I can help. We'll put a ceiling of five hundred on it. If, at the end of the five hundred, the case is still dragging, I'll refer you to another, less expensive attorney." I agreed. This man knew and was known by everyone in the city's domestic court scene. He was known and respected by the opposing attorney. He proceeded to apply just the right amount of pressure at the appropriate times in the appropriate places. In brief, four hundred and forty dollars later, I was divorced. I was to pay neither alimony nor a cash settlement, and I had full custody of our only child. I realized then that when an expert is operating in his own field of endeavor and knows "where to tap the pipe," forty dollars an hour is very inexpensive indeed.

Recalling this episode, I took the bull by the horns and decided that my fee would be forty dollars an hour. I must admit that I choked or mumbled the first few times I quoted it, but because of credentials, I was delighted and surprised to find that no one laughed. Concomitantly, I quoted two hundred dollars per day. I now boast a file of letters from satisfied clients who tell me (as I told my attorney years ago) that, in the face of the help they derived from my work, I am inexpensive.

I did not raise my fees for the first five years. When it became necessary to do so (because time constraints no longer permitted me to work at that price), I did some homework beforehand and I came up with an excellent rule-of-thumb. The "homework" I refer to was in the form of questioning my most long term clients with regard to their psychology of paying my fees and getting their truthful feedback. It seems that no one minds paying me an hourly fee that is ten dollars less than that of the psychoanalyst (not psychologist) in my area. So in hindsight I realized that at the time that I charged $40 per hour, they were $50 per hour. I now charge $65 per hour. When they go to $100 per hour, I'll go to $90. Don't ask me why this is so; it just is. On a daily basis, my fee is seven times the hourly fee; the client expects a break, and he gets it in the form of that one free hour. Concomitantly, my weekly fee is four times the daily fee.

I have no doubt that this fee set-up will work for anyone in any field, because many of my consultant clients have tried it with enormous success.

But in the beginning, all was not roses. You will discover that if you are highly recommended by another client or someone who knows you, the prospect will never question your fee. However, if you are dealing with someone who has never heard of you, your fee arouses suspicion. Wanting very much to work, your first impulse will be to lower your fee for that prospect who is "from Missouri." Instinct told me not to, and I didn't. Don't you ever do it, either. It will hurt your reputation and your credibility. I learned that the questioning of the fee was just a smokescreen for the questioning of my expertise, since they had never heard of me. You could cut your fee in half at this juncture, and it would do no good. Once your credentials, your expertise in their problem area, and your general experience are all established, there is never flak about your fee. The client merely wants to be assured that you can help him. You can supply this assurance by talking knowledgeably about similar cases in general and about his case in particular. But never make the mistake of cutting your fees. Conversely, never increase your fee just because you might think that your prospective client is a "fat cat" and that you've got him snowed. A major part of the "credentials" I keep talking about is your reputation, your integrity, and the ethical standards you set for yourself. It is a strange psychological phenomenon, but if you know yourself to be an ethical person and an honest one, you will come across that way to the prospect at the first meeting. If you know that you are a bit shady and greedy, he will know it, too.

Now perhaps you can benefit from a big mistake that I did make in this matter of fees. A prospect would call and request an exploratory meeting with me to discuss his problems or a particular project. "Fine," I bellowed over the phone, "my fee is forty dollars an hour." I was remembering all the signs I had come across in doctors' and dentists' offices warning that the patients should discuss fees in advance so that there is no embarrassment later. No soap. The prospect invariably got upset with me then and there. His general reaction went something like this: "You expect me to pay you in order to find out whether or not I want to do business with you? You must be nuts." Well, this cropped up again and again for several months, while I stupidly and stubbornly stuck to my guns. Then two things dawned on me. First, I was losing good potential business. Second, the parallels between the consultant and the doctor ended right there. I put myself in the caller's place; he was right, of course. Thereafter, I simply postponed the fee quotation until that point in the first meeting at which it seemed that we might work together, or until he asked. It worked; but, more important, I worked. Even when it didn't work, I had accomplished something almost as important; I had made another professional contact and added that name to my Wheeldex.

These exploratory meetings can be tricky. From time to time, you will come across someone who will try to use this as a freebie to pump valuable information from you. He is the same person who will attempt to discuss his gall bladder condition with the first physician he meets at a cocktail party. Again the professional parallel falls apart here. The physician merely tells this joker to make an appointment at his office through his nurse. You, on the other hand, must give away a few "free samples." It is the only way to show your wares. If done deftly, he will come away from the meeting with the full realization that you have only scratched the surface of his situation, that although impressive, the information you gave him is worthless by itself, and that he would do well to pay you to learn more.

Here are a few rules that now govern my fees, and that I came to trust after painful experience:

1. I never waive my fee—for anyone. The few times in the beginning that I did, I was sorry. Not placing a value on my time, the client considered it valueless in every instance. He therefore ignored whatever my input. He invariably failed in his project. And guess who he told everyone "helped" him with his project? That's right; I was the consultant on the job.
2. I never swap my fee or barter it for someone else's services. One party or the other always feels he is getting the short end of the stick.
3. I never work on a contingency fee basis. This is described in full later in this chapter.
4. In charging a client for expenses, I charge only for those expenses incurred out of town. I never charge him for that part of my office rent, my assistant's time, or my telephone that could be costed out to the project. I would like to explain this, since it is my understanding that I am the only consultant who works this way. Whether I had two projects or twenty, I would maintain my office, my phone and my assistant in any event. It has always seemed unfair to charge a client for any of these items. As far as he is concerned, I could work alone at home.
5. I didn't raise my fees for five years, despite the rising costs of doing business. Every consultant in good health is capable of working at least forty hours a week for fifty-two weeks out of the year. In my case, this would have amounted to a gross annual income of $83,200. I would have liked very much to have earned this amount doing consulting work, but I didn't. More impor-

tant, I would have liked to have worked that much, because it's so enjoyable. So why cut down on the amount of work by raising the price and scaring a lot of small clients away?

The Contingency Fee

The contingency fee is one that is paid to the professional only if the project ends in success for the client. A flat fee, on the other hand, is paid by the client, win, lose, or draw. So all clients prefer a contingency fee. Most professionals accept contingency-fee arrangements from time to time.

I am the only consultant I know who will never accept a fee on a contingency basis. The reasons for this are basic to the way I work and to my fundamental attitude toward that work.

The amount of the contingency fee is invariably pegged to a percentage of the client's ultimate financial success in the project or venture. Ofttimes, however, this single project's immediate monetary return is at odds with the long-term goals of the company or even with the success of that project itself. I am as human as the next person, which means that I like money. If I were to work on a contingency fee basis and had to advise my client to choose one of several offers regarding a project, I'm not so sure that I would elect the most beneficial one every time. I would probably point to the one with the most money involved, since that would give me the biggest fee. In another instance, I could well advise the client to take the first offer that came along, regardless of its merits, in order to conclude that project and get my fee as quickly as possible. I am, after all, selling my time.

Back to the comparison with the lawyer. A consultant has no more idea in advance of how long a project will take than does a lawyer. Things do have a way of dragging on. Not long ago, an attorney I had engaged on a contingency fee basis urged me to accept a $2500 settlement on a $72,500 lawsuit because the case had already been in negotiation for over a year and he got fed up. His fee was $750. I really felt that he hadn't served my best interests, since it was he who had convinced me to sue for the original amount in the first place.

Serving the best interests of the client is the ultimate "report card." Making a fast buck is deleterious to your career and to your self-esteem.

Here are two case histories that exemplify how I work in this regard. I choose them because in each of them, I came out on different ends of the financial stick.

A local organization called me because it was trying to make a business arrangement with my former company. I was requested to go out of town to the company headquarters, have lunch with a vice-president who was a former co-worker, and convince her to accept the deal. I told the client immediately that success was dubious in this instance due to the company's policies, which were adverse to this kind of proposition. He insisted on retaining me to try. He offered me $5,000 if I succeeded. I calmly quoted my fee for the day plus expenses. He was aghast. "Man, I'm offering you five grand for one day's work, and you talk peanuts. How can you think so small?" Well, my thinking went something like this: If I accept his offer and I fail, I'm out of pocket over a hundred dollars in expenses; if I succeed, the fee is unfair because no one is worth $5,000 for a day's work. What he heard from me was simply, "Those are my fees." I was retained, I made the pitch as best I could, and the offer was turned down by my former colleague, as I had predicted. I was duly paid by the client. He later tried other means but failed.

The second case involves a project that reeked of success from its inception. I knew immediately what I could do and how I would do it. Had I at that time requested one percent of the project's eventual receipts, all the parties involved would have jumped at the offer. But I didn't. I was retained at my daily fee. I brought the project to a successful conclusion in two full working days. It eventually brought the clients $400,000 in revenues. Can't you just see my accountant screaming at me in a frenzy? He did. What kind of idiot opts for $800 instead of $4,000? The kind of idiot who is writing this book. First of all, no one could tell what the ultimate revenues would be for that project (or any other). Second, the reason I worked so effectively is that I was unhampered by my own possible greed. I therefore connected smoothly and quickly with those organizations that I knew would be most amenable and efficient with regard to that project. I still feel good about that one. And let's not forget the income derived from the subsequent clients who heard about this project on the grapevine, and the additional work given to me by the original client.

I remember my mother saying when I was a small child, "How do you know you don't want to eat it if you don't taste it?" Yes, I tried a contingency fee once, just to satisfy my bewildered and irate accountant. Hence my adamancy on this subject. This is what happened:

A client came to me with a project because he wanted me to present it to another client. Client A offered me ten percent of the deal, if consummated. I accepted. The following day I closed the deal. Client B gave client A a check for $15,000. Well, I thought, perhaps I have been missing the boat after all. On the following day, client B reconsidered and put a "stop" on the check to client

A—a bad practice, I agree; nevertheless, he did it. I kept my fee because I had done my part and because client A sued client B and won. Needless to say, I lost both clients. Had I returned the fee, it wouldn't have helped because there was so much bad feeling all around. Upon self-scrutinizing reflection, I realized that, because of the contingency-fee arrangement, I behaved differently in this case than I ever had before. I had taken this project to the first people I knew would jump at it, particularly if they thought it was a bargain. I had also concluded the deal at the first and lowest offer. I did not deliberate whether it was in the best interests of the project itself to put these two clients together. The fact that client B had second thoughts after I left his office bears all of this out. In truth, I saw a fast $1,500 flashing in neon lights before my eyes during this entire matter. I don't know; maybe I shouldn't have kept the fee after all.

I am convinced that whatever good reputation I have is partially based on the fact that I do not accept contingency fee arrangements.

Chapter Seven

Money

Adjusted for inflation, here is a picture of my gross receipts for the first five years of my free-lancing and consulting. This is on a calendar-year basis:

First year	$ 18,000
Second year	$ 44,000
Third year	$ 66,000
Fourth year	$ 92,000
Fifth year	$102,000

My first year as an independent produced only one-half the annual income I had earned in my former job. But, along with the advantage of new-found freedom, one must also consider the many tax advantages of being self-employed. There are absolutely none while working for someone else, as you well know.

The curve did not continue to rise in the same manner for the subsequent five years, as far as my consulting work was concerned. I was, however, in a position to take financial part in several ventures in my industry to which

I was exposed in my capacity as a consultant, and I was quick to seize the opportunities.

In the third year, I found that I could not sustain the work load alone, and I hired an assistant. I use the word "assistant" advisedly, because I did not then, and do not now need a secretary. I find that it takes twice as much time to dictate a letter to a secretary and have her type it as it does to sit down at a typewriter myself and complete the letter in one motion. My right index finger is not arthritic, so I am also perfectly capable of dialing the telephone myself. Besides, I cannot abide the ludicrous game that secretaries play with each other to the tune of "Put your Mr. X on, and then I'll put my Mr. Y on." And here again, I have never lost any "image" by answering my own phone or not having secretarial initials on the bottom of my letters.

After much interviewing, I decided on someone who had never worked in the business world before, hence hadn't picked up any bad working habits. I wanted a *tabula rasa*, so I hired a young lady fresh out of graduate school, who commended herself to me by dint of the facts that: she came from a fine family, she had a good working knowledge of the English language, and although she could type only slowly she could proofread her work accurately and was somewhat of a perfectionist. She also had an excellent telephone voice. Most of all, she was intelligent, trustworthy, eager, and a rapid learner. Her starting salary was only somewhat above the minimum wage. Within two years she was earning fifty percent more. Within four years, her salary doubled.

My assistant's work consisted mainly of back-up details: a certain amount of bookkeeping, the handling of the mail, and the knowledgeable running of the office when I was out of town. She was always totally aware of everything that went on in the office. The main reason for this was my having had the dividing wall torn down two years before. She was privy to every conversation, phone call, and written communication. In short order, my clients came to know her and trust her. She is no longer in my employ because, unfortunately, a consultant's assistant is not an assistant consultant. No client would seek, or pay for, her advice. So it was a dead-end job, and she ultimately went on to better things.

But, back to money. There are two ways to have it. One way is to earn it. The other way is not to spend it. If you can do both, you will wind up with twice as much. I was earning enough to buy an expensive car (I use my car exclusively for business), to move my office into the fashionable end of town, to install expensive furniture and equipment, and even to hire a second person. I was advised that the Internal Revenue Service would actually be paying for a goodly percentage of this anyhow. But I neither needed nor had any desire for any of those things. I liked my old car; we had become friends. Certainly there was no new building in the swank section of town that allowed me the privilege of opening or closing a window or turning on the air conditioner on a hot off-season day, much less bringing my dog to work. And one with a real fireplace? I was comfortable in my office as it was. As for an additional employee, I use a "temporary" on the few occasions when the workload is that heavy. To the contrary, I kept heading in the other direction; when I costed out the Xerox machine I had rented against individual copies at the instant print shop downstairs, I returned the machine. Superfluity of any kind is wasteful.

Elizabeth Seton once advised "Live simply so that others may simply live." That is both true and noble. But my working life is kept simple so that I may simply live another day. My income is neither guaranteed nor steady. Neither is my good health assured forever. Not spending profligately nor taxing my small business inordinately because of personal desires for needless luxuries gives me the ultimate luxury: peace of mind and the assurance that I will always have an office. Besides, the Internal Revenue Service actually pays for nothing. It would be my fellow citizens who would be paying for my impetuousness—and that's not fair.

A word about temporary help. Employment agencies that specialize in this kind of work are amazingly good, as a general rule. They are uncanny in the way they rate and categorize their people. For a low hourly fee, you will get a fairly dull, but conscientious, unskilled person. For twice that amount, you will get one of the brightest, skilled, and most capable people you ever came across. This is someone who cannot abide the humdrum life of going to the same office and doing the same things all her life, but thrives on diversity. Then you have all the accurate gradations in between. All, however, are eager and willing to work, and I have never known any to take advantage of the temporary employer. Most important, there is absolutely no waste. The very moment the job is completed, the person is dismissed and you stop paying.

I am probably representing myself as Scrooge incarnate. That is only part of the picture. I do let loose the financial reins in some aspects of my work, for example, business lunches and other forms of business entertainment, business trips not paid for by clients, and long-distance telephone calls. Indeed, anything that will open the lines of communication between my office and the outside world, I find worth spending for.

Approximately two-fifths of my annual revenue is spent on the cost of doing business as a consultant. This puts me into a fairly high tax bracket for a little guy. But, after paying Uncle Sam, I find that I have more than enough left to live very well by any standards and still keep "a little something" left over.

Most important, I have no debts. I pay all of my bills on the day I receive them. Try that sometime for peace of mind. Conversely, I bill all clients within two days after my service is performed. I then meticulously follow up all invoices with monthly statements and phone calls. Since I have been both flat broke and comparatively well off in a short period of time, I am very comfortable about money and have absolutely no embarrassment about asking for it from anyone who owes it to me for an undue length of time. Money just isn't a dirty word in my vocabulary. As a result, out of a total billing for the first ten years of over $800,000, I have collected all except $65—and I'd have gotten to that deadbeat if he hadn't skipped to California. My accountant was incredulous and assured me that this must be some kind of all-time record. Maybe it is.

Chapter Eight

Consulting, At Last

It was exactly ten months after I had set myself up, established my hourly fee, and had been working on long-term projects for monthly retainers, that I abruptly started to do actual consulting. I received three telephone inquiries within one week. Two of them were from individuals who had found my name in the Yellow Pages. The third was from the executive director of a large association; he had heard about me from someone I had never met (this has happened a number of times). In all three cases, I asked them to identify the general nature of their problems on the phone. All confirmed appointments for three different days.

A word about those Yellow Pages. I have never placed an advertisement in them. I simply have the regular listing to which I am entitled by dint of the fact that I have a phone. Over the years, I have averaged one inquiry per week from this source.

I must confess that, unbeknownst to the client, I experienced extreme "stage fright" before each of these meetings. What would they ask? What vast stores of knowledge was I supposed to be the repository of? What if their problems dealt with subjects and areas I had never been exposed to and that were beyond my expertise? In short, what if I didn't have the answers? Forty dollars an hour! Big shot! Now I was on the proverbial spot. What do I do if they ask ten questions and I can answer only five? Refund twenty dollars? How many people in what short period of time would they tell that I was a fraud?

Well, my friend was right, of course. We don't know how much we know. The sessions went smoothly and professionally. Without any specific preparation (impossible because I didn't know the actual questions in advance), I was both knowledgeable and erudite in every instance. The clients were pleasantly surprised at the amount of useful information they received in one hour's time. No, I didn't stretch it out to increase my fee. I had something to prove to them and to myself—that I was a bargain. And I did. This stage fright did not end after those three sessions. It cropped up again and again for two more years. Not always. Just in those instances where I had forgotten how much experience I really had. Always, this uneasiness left me within the first five minutes of the consultation.

So, above my regular income that week, I earned another $120 for three hours of work. The most pleasant and exhilarating work I had ever done. A taste of blood, so to speak. I wanted more, much more of this. I realized, though, that, just like those first three, the rest would have to come in of their own accord. There was nothing I could do to push it, rush it, or in any way make it happen. I was then unaware of the two-step marketing method described in Chapter 15. The only thing I did then was carefully add those three names to my Wheeldex. Over the years, I have sent these people and those who followed some unusual communication at Christmastime to remind them that I am still here should they ever need my services again.

I did one thing, however, which helped me as I went along. I printed up a partial list of clients (see back of the book). Partial because I only listed the more familiar and notable names. As the list grew, so did my credibility as a consultant with prospective clients. Now whenever I present my calling card, I also proffer my list. I have the list lengthened and reprinted every six months.

My consultancy started to pyramid. With that, my reputation pyramided, too. Requests started to trickle in for me to speak about my industry before small groups. At first, I jumped at the chance to do this free of charge. Later, as the groups became larger, I required an honorarium. Additional requests came in for me to write articles in trade publications. Here again, I started without benefit of fee and later charged for it. The Mark Twain syndrome was repeating itself, in a sense.

All of this activity brought the yearned-for additional consulting work. Two years after those first phone calls, my consulting work accounted for fifty percent of my revenue. I had arrived.

Chapter Nine

Contracts

I am the only consultant I ever heard of who absolutely refuses to enter into any legal contractual agreement with a client. As a consequence, this cannot be a chapter on how to write an airtight contract. Rather, I would hope to make you understand why I shun them. Perhaps I can convince you to do likewise.

It is most often the consultant who tries to get the client to sign a contract, not the other way around. The client is usually shy of this. What if the consultant doesn't produce, proves himself inept somewhere down the line, becomes lazy, misses meetings or writes an unintelligible final report? The client would be stuck. So, pragmatically, pushing a contract into a client's face and trying to force him to use legal counsel to make a deal with you simply cuts your chances of working in half. Let us assume, however, that a one-year contract is signed by the client, engaging your services. You are now married to each other. The first two months comprise the honeymoon. You are the darling of the company. Everyone is running around, pointing you out as the genius who is going to solve all of their problems, eliminate their competition, and make them a huge success. After all, they have a contract. Let us even assume that you are indeed good enough to accomplish this insane one-year goal. It will take you some time, even though you are a genius, to get started. It takes a couple of months just to get acquainted with how the client has been doing things wrong. His middle management will constantly try to hide it from you. You invoice them monthly, because this is the usual procedure and the only sensible one. By the end of the third month, they still haven't conquered the world and they see no tangible progress. A bit of the heartiness goes out of their greetings in the morning. You are not slapped quite so hard on the back anymore. You are invited to fewer meetings. They become somewhat soured by the fact that your monthly invoices are going to be arriving like clockwork for the next nine months, and as yet they have nothing concrete to show for their money. They are finding it just a bit difficult to justify your presence and your expense to their controller. In short, the honeymoon is over. You are stuck with each other. You are grudgingly going to their meetings, and they are grudgingly paying your invoices. The relationship should terminate right here, but it can't. There is a contract, and the first one to even suggest termination is "in breach." Then it becomes bitter. They may lose some more money, but you lose reputation—and the work is no longer enjoyable.

Here is another reason to eschew contracts. A consultant is not a TV repairman. The work is neither that precise nor that cut-and-dried. But even a TV repairman will not quote a price for his work until he sees exactly what is wrong with the set. You do not have that opportunity on any long-range project. You go into a contractual agreement with absolutely no idea of how much of your time it will eventually take, what political internal obstacles you will meet, how many meetings a week your client will require you to attend, and what tangential business of theirs you must familiarize yourself with to accomplish their goals. Your retainer is only a wild guess at best on your part. You could well be required to put in so much time that you come out having earned an average of $3.50 an hour by the end of the year or whatever the contractual period. Without a contract the fee may be renegotiated anywhere along the line by either party, up or down. The consultant/client relationship has a much better chance of thriving.

Again, suppose you start working and find that your client is involved in practices that are against your moral principles. If you signed a contract, you are stuck.

It has always seemed to me that contracts are entrapments. Remember, you chose the career of consulting to avoid being trapped in life ever again. Now you are back where you started. Let's return to the professional parallel with the doctor, dentist, or psychiatrist. No property is being negotiated here, just as in your case. If one person needs help and the other person is willing and capable of giving it, who needs lawyers, legal contracts, and their attendant expense? If a prospective client insists on it, I automatically don't trust him. The only time it is ever necessary to sign a contract is when you do work for any government agency on any level.

With regard to long-term or ongoing projects, here is what I do. I always request and get a letter of intent from the individual client or responsible executive representing an organization. In this letter is a general description of the work required of me and the monthly fee to be paid. There is also a sentence that states that either party may terminate this arrangement with thirty days of prior notice to the other. Prospects are very pleasantly surprised to come upon such an arrangement. When I proffer it, they look upon me as being guileless, which I am. They are also more easily able to enter into such an agreement because it does not require a large figure entry into the annual budget beforehand, and therefore doesn't require approval from a superior, controller, or board of directors. Recall that my very first client retained me for over six years on this basis.

The strangest and nicest thing about this letter of intent (which I request be no more than one page long) is that it is, in effect, legally binding. I had an unfortunate incident in which this legality was tested. Here is what happened.

One of the largest professional associations in the country called upon me to do a study concerning the feasibility of a project. My study proved the project feasible. The executive in charge of the division called me in and asked if I would like to administer the project on a freelance basis. I agreed and quoted my fee annually, since I knew exactly how much time would be required in this case. He accepted with the proviso that I waive my fee for the feasibility study. I agreed to this, too, because I liked both the man and the project. I requested my usual letter of intent setting all of this forth on one page in simple language. The letter arrived the following day. I immediately started work. Several weeks later, this man was promoted to another division, and another man moved into his place. This second individual called me into his office, thanked me for what I had done, and informed me that the association could very well proceed without me. I quickly turned the letter of intent over to my attorney, who sued forthwith on the strength of that letter. The matter was settled out of court, and the client paid me $10,000.

I rest my case concerning contracts.

Chapter Ten

The Work

A consultant's work is so wondrously varied that it would be impossible to categorize or describe the assignments that have come to me and will come to you. However, since "the impossible takes only a little longer" I shall attempt it.

You will be asked how to accomplish any task in any facet of your industry in the most expeditious and economical way. Thereafter, you may be asked to actually do the work yourself. If you demur on the second part, you are an ivory-tower-beard-stroking consultant. If not, you are a working consultant. The working consultant is usually busier, earns more money (it's the same hourly fee whether you work or talk), gains a better reputation faster, and has the confidence of the client by dint of the fact that he is willing to put into practice what he has preached, rather than pontificate and run.

You will be asked for pure, hard, current information dealing with your profession or industry. You must either have this information at hand or be familiar with the referential sources from which you can glean it. These sources may repose in an extensive library in your office or in a public library or both. Your primary requisite for this kind of consulting is the careful reading of every respected trade or professional publication in your field. Your clients generally don't have the time to do this. You must make the time.

There is a big secondary benefit to extensive reading. It will save you lots of time and money; remember that now time and money are the same in your work. You will get a complete overview plus all the "meat" of any seminar, lecture, or convention you thought you might attend for your own educational purposes. Ofttimes the concepts will present themselves more clearly by reading about them in your chosen surroundings than by actually attending these meetings. Seminars, meetings, and conventions are obscured and obfuscated by booze, hullabaloo, stupid questions, fatigue, and agenda items that insult your intelligence and experience. Of course, if you just want to take a tax-deductible trip to get away from it all, that is a different matter. Also, good contacts can sometimes be made at conventions to which prospective clients in your field may throng. Generally, however, you can accomplish more for yourself and for your clients by staying home and "tending your garden," reading all the while. Once in a while, you may be asked to attend a convention in your client's behalf for your regular fee; that is a convention not to be missed.

You will be asked to make a pitch or present a deal for a client. Why doesn't he use one of his salesmen or do it himself? Because he is smart. Coming from you the deal has more credibility and sincerity. Besides, the one to be pitched to may be another one of your clients or just someone in the field who has confidence in you.

You will be asked to do a feasibility study on a project the client would like to undertake but for which he wants outside objective reassurance. Conversely, you will be asked to do a similar study because the client does *not* want to take a particular course of action and wants to present an unbiased, independent report to his board of directors; he wants this report to tell them that the project in question is foolhardy and the executive in charge is not merely lazy. In either case, never accept an assignment in which the client tells you beforehand the conclusions he wants. It may force you to fudge and lie—a detriment to your reputation and integrity.

You will be asked to recommend a candidate to fill a sensitive job opening. Conversely you will be asked if you know of any job opportunities. Be careful here. Never recommend either way, unless you know the job is suited to the person and vice versa. Again, your reputation is on the line. Never accept or request a fee for this service (unless of course you are a personnel consultant). If you are able to handle this form of request (gratis) expertly and to the satisfaction of both parties, your reward will come in the form of consulting work from this quarter further down the line, out of respect and gratitude.

You will be asked to sit in on a brainstorming session just because you have a good mind and because you are objective. The purpose here is to have you come up with some ideas that the other attendees may miss because they are too close to the situation and "cannot see the forest for the trees." You will be asked to carry out a job or a chore that the client thought up but is too lazy to do himself. An exaggerated, ludicrous, but true example of this is the time a client paid me my hourly fee to take a bunch of mail to the post office and have every piece registered.

Getting to the periphery of this subject, if your client is located out of town, you may be asked to entertain a V.I.P. while he or she is in your city.

Finally, you will be asked to write reports about everything: feasibility studies, progress, regress, methodology, budgets, what you think, what your client thinks, the state of the industry, and personnel evaluation. You should be able to write concisely and clearly in an organized way with a good command of the language.

Believe it or not, all of the above will take up about half of your time. Another 25 percent of your time should be taken up in the constant pursuit of new business, that is, marketing. Treat your marketing function as though it were a permanent client on permanent retainer. The remaining 25 percent of the time is where the real creative part comes in.

It isn't just that you should never stop thinking. It's that you should never stop doing. Doing what? Doing what you are thinking about. You have heard the expression "Ideas are a dime a dozen." Not true. Ideas are a nickel a gross. Ideas, in fact, are worthless unless someone does something about them. Most of us at one time or another have asked "Why don't they do something about _____?" Who are "they?" Why don't you? Well, that is what I do with the other 25 percent of my time. I'm constantly musing about how my profession can be improved, and continuously trying to come up with ways to make those improvements happen. Whenever I get an idea that seems sound, I pick up the phone and call a respected executive with clout, make an appointment, and tell him my idea. Almost everyone will talk with a consultant gratis. By the way, I am not anal retentive about these ideas; as we discovered, by themselves they are worthless anyhow. At this point, one of several things will happen:

1. The person across the desk will clap me on the back, tell me that I'm a genius, adopt or adapt the idea for his firm and dismiss me. Always remember, no one pays for unrequested ideas.
2. He will accept the idea and ask me to carry it out for him for a fee. Or

3. He will tell me that my brainchild is unworkable and give me sixteen good reasons why. Whereupon, I will either fold my tent or go back to the drawing board. Or
4. He will reinforce my idea but tell me that he is just too lazy or too busy to do anything about it.

If it is "4" and my idea requires a fair-sized investment of capital, I'll take it to others who are not lazy or too busy. If it doesn't require much money, but only a whole lot of work, I will immediately set about doing it myself. After all, I have the time (which equates to money) and the know-how and the contacts.

Let me cite two examples of how this has worked for me. It is worth taking the time to go into this in some detail because this is the creative, innovative area of consulting work that you don't normally read or hear about.

One evening I was sitting in the theatre waiting for the curtain to rise, when something caught my eye in the program. "Why don't they _____?" I thought. The next morning I telephoned the executive vice-president of the company in question. He listened for a few minutes and invited me to come and visit him. When I arrived, he dismissed my idea forthwith explaining that he had tried that a few years before and it hadn't worked. But he was intrigued by my phone call, by the fact that we both had the same idea albeit several years apart, and by my assertiveness in calling him personally. Now it happened that he needed a consultant regarding another matter, and that was the real reason he asked me to visit. I was retained for three months to accomplish his task. The job was done in two months.

One year later, I was lying on the beach, and an idea for a totally unique marketing method came to me. I spoke with five different company principals about it.

Mind you, I was giving it away! I just wanted to see it done. All were enthused, but none would do anything about it. I sold a few acres of country property I had acquired two years before. Armed with this money, my marketing scheme, and the previous enthusiasm of my do-nothing colleagues, I set up a small company to do it myself. Within six months, the plan netted $22,000. I was satisfied. It worked. That is all I really cared about. I did not want to continue to run that business and give up my life of freedom. I went to one of my clients and sold that enterprise for $75,000.

I am still doing this kind of thing. Not all of my ideas are workable. The point is that whenever I get an idea, I concomitantly have a surging need to know whether or not it will work, in the same way that a composer needs to hear his latest work performed. I keep a file called "ideas." I fully intend to prove or disprove every one of them before I die.

I have one other method of accumulating work. Whenever I plan a trip anywhere over two thousand miles, whether on vacation, in my own professional behalf, or on assignment for a client, I send a letter to all of my clients informing them of this. In this letter I ask if there is any task or errand they would like me to perform for them in that faraway place. Invariably, I get some positive response. You see, the client immediately realizes that the biggest part of the expense—fare, hotels, and meals—are already paid for. If he has something to be done in that distant city that would take only two hours, it will cost him only $130. It certainly doesn't pay for him to send one of his people or go himself at those rates. You would be surprised at how many of my trips have been subsidized in this manner. Do these odd jobs put a crimp in my trip? Not at all. I love my work.

Time and again, a client who is impressed with your work and your know-how will offer you a lucrative, full-time executive position in his company. These offers are tempting, but you will have to muster all of your will power and refuse them. Otherwise, you will lose your hard-won freedom. Besides, you would not be nearly as effective back in the table of organization as you are now in your independent state. Your job-offering client doesn't realize this, but you must.

Chapter Eleven

The Proposal

There are books on how to write a proposal, and there are books on how to write a report. But for the consultant, these books as separate entities are meaningless. In our profession, the proposal and the report are linked in so many ways that they virtually become one process. Indeed, the success or failure of a consulting assignment ofttimes hinges on the connection between the initial proposal and the final report. Hence these chapters, which treat the two as a unified whole.

The formerly accepted styles and forms of proposal and report writing are quickly becoming passe. Astute executives and businessmen are getting fed up with them; as prospective clients, their jaundiced eyes are beginning to look upon most of this noncommunicative effort as garbage. Those consultants and consulting firms that still use the old format do so because they don't ask for feedback; they submit, bill, and run. These two chapters are the result of the answers I received when I asked a number of clients (my own and others'), "What did you think of the proposal (or report)?" We shall deal with the writing of effective proposals and effective reports. Effective proposals are those which succeed in obtaining the work desired by the consultant for his normal fee. Effective reports are those that succeed in satisfying the client that the consultant's work was properly and professionally accomplished; they also succeed by the consultant's getting paid.

The need for this is apparent when we see the number of proposals that are rejected and the number of reports that are either misunderstood or treated with indifference. A proposal that does not eventuate in a client retaining the consultant wastes an enormous amount of time—for both parties; and this time translates into money. Likewise, a report that doesn't accomplish what it set out to do, or obfuscates its own intent, both infuriates and loses clients.

Time and money wasted is injurious to any profession, but for a consultant it is doubly so, because this waste is always obvious to the client and cannot be hidden in any way.

For the wise consultant, the consideration of whether to write a proposal starts very early. He differentiates between a prospect and a suspect, between a winner and a loser. Similarly, the consideration of what kind of report to write should start long before it is written—in the solid consultant/client relationship, whereby the client is fully aware and expectant of the type of report you will write. Everything comes together if, as Holiday Inn suggests, there are no surprises.

This is not a manual of style or of creative writing. For that you are referred to "The Elements of Style" by Strunk and White. It is, however, a guide to do's and don'ts based upon my own experience. The general rules here transcend all fields of consulting, so that, whatever your expertise, you should find them useful.

When to Write a Proposal

Every field is filled with time wasters, wheel spinners, and losers. Whether or not these people (and many are to be found in high executive positions) waste your time or spin your wheels is entirely up to you. It takes two to tango. In most cases, the smart consultant will set up an exploratory meeting with a potential client before taking on any assignment. The foolish consultant will rush in and accept an assignment without knowing enough about it or the client. Nor is a slack period any excuse. You will have only yourself to blame if:

1. the client doesn't pay your fee,
2. the client is involved in something shady or illegal,
3. the client is "using" you for purposes other than the ostensible assignment, or
4. the client claims later on that he wasn't sure of your terms or your fees.

So the first meeting is very important from many points of view. From the very beginning, pay attention. Have you been kept waiting long beyond your appointed time? This could be a signal that the potential client is a time waster—yours or his, it makes no difference; it could be a signal that he is inconsiderate and has little regard for the fact that you have things to do other than read magazines in his outer office. (Of course, sometimes his excuse may be valid.)

Next, is this person trying to get a free session with you under the guise of an exploratory meeting? You can determine this by the specificity of his questions. Also, even though it would appear that he is interviewing you, you should be deftly interviewing him at the same time. Find out whether he is considering any other consultant for the job, whether he is shopping for price alone, or whether he is merely using you and/or your subsequent proposal to bring another consultant "in line." I don't know about others, but I have found it extremely difficult to charge a client for a proposal. He seems to have every right on his side when he objects to the fact that I would charge him for the time it takes me to convince him to retain me (which is what a proposal is). But most often, the proposal shows the consultant in the best light by offering innovative methodology for problem-solving. Savvy clients who know this could act on the proposals without retaining the consultant. These proposals are neither copyrighted nor the exclusive property of the consultant, once submitted. So the proposal can be the first piece of solid advice offered to the prospective client, and I never offer to write one unless I am more than 90 percent certain that the client is "for real." The most direct method I use for ascertaining the seriousness of the prospective client's intentions is confronting him or her outright. I ask:

> When do you propose to start on this project?
> Are you properly funded for it?
> When do you expect to have this project completed?
> To whom would I report?
> Who will be working with me? Who can answer any quesions I might have? Etc.

All of these questions are well calculated to make the prospect understand that I am not fooling around.

Beware of the executive who calls you in and requests a proposal, outlining not only the problems but the solutions as well. He is usually trying to convince another member of his organization or board of directors that he is right—and wants to use the documentation of "an outside impartial consultant" to prove his point. Nothing more. He has no intention of retaining you.

Finally, I am wary of the prospect who uses this meeting for trivial or personal talk.

You can spot a "live" prospect when he or she is forthcoming about the task ahead, about the organization's problems to be solved, and about what is expected of the consultant in this instance. If it is a miracle worker they want, withdraw (unless you have been successfully walking on water lately). If the person sitting on the other side of the desk from you seems to know the problems, articulates them well, and doesn't pridefully try to cover them up, you would do well to offer a proposal. It is always a pleasure to do business with someone who knows his business. On the other hand, if the executive is obviously inept, he won't understand a good proposal anyhow—so why bother?

Another clue I use is the due date offered for receipt of my proposal. If he needs it "yesterday," then the entire project will be an impossibility, and, once again, I withdraw. Conversely, if he has no due date at all, then he is not taking the project seriously in the first place, and we are merely chatting about nothing.

But whenever you have any kind of positive feeling about the client and/or the project, *always* offer a proposal, even if the client demurs. Remember that your proposal is your greatest sales opportunity and the only real chance you have to exhibit your expertise.

What Kind of Proposal?

At first glance, it would appear that a consultant should tailor his writing to the taste of the client. Not so. If a client is a devious type who beats about the bush, this is no reason to write a monograph that accommodates his nature. He will spot what you are doing right off anyway, because it takes one to know one. All proposals and reports should be straightforward and to the point.

But there are different kinds of proposals with respect to what it is that the consultant hopes to achieve. For example:

1. The entire project itself may be the writing of a report, in which you will divest yourself of everything you know about that type of problem. In this case, the proposal will merely be a restatement of your credentials and expertise in this area, a general idea of what your report will contain, a quotation of your fee, and a due date for the report.
2. The project could call for a long-term contract (or letter of intent) for your services on an ongoing basis. Here the proposal would generalize about what it is that you would do for your client, the goals, and the areas in which you intend to accomplish this. Needless to say, this proposal would be much more detailed and lengthy than the former one.
3. The client may request a budgeting proposal. This could call for a definitive explanation of the project along with the costs (in addition to your fee) for carrying out the work entailed and/or the price to the client if he were to pay you on a cost-plus basis, that is, not conducting the project in-house.

You can readily see that, in length alone, these would be three different kinds of proposals. How long should a proposal or report be? As long as it takes to write it—and write it well! Writing can be the most precise method of communication. But precision and brevity are not always synonymous. Write concisely and to the point. But don't leave anything out just for the sake of brevity. Most writers see a contradiction between brevity and comprehensiveness. There is none. A twenty-page treatise dealing with a complicated matter may be considered just as concise and succinct as a two-page document dealing with a simple matter.

There is only one instance that calls for extreme brevity. Once in a while it requires the decision of a committee or board of directors to okay your services. The person conducting your exploratory interview is merely screening. Always request that you address this group personally. A go-between trying to sell your services rarely succeeds. This for two reasons: first, he is not as intensely enthusiastic as you are regarding this matter; second, the board will raise the most simplistic questions, which he cannot answer and you can. Invariably, when a sufficient number of unanswered questions crop up, the entire matter is either shelved until the next meeting or dropped altogether. If you are prohibited from attending the meeting, your proposal must speak for you. Several days or the night before the meeting, each member receives your proposal along with a raft of material pertaining to other items on the agenda. The members are supposed to digest all of this in preparation for the meeting. They rarely do. The shorter the piece, the more they are apt to at least glance at it. So brevity here is your only chance.

Style

Despite what you may hear or read to the contrary, there is no single acceptable writing style for proposals and reports. All kinds of submissions have garnered clients for consultants—and have been rejected as well.

It must be assumed, of course, that you have total command of the written English language—with all that this entails: syntax, grammar, punctuation, spelling, etc.

Furthermore, you need a vocabulary sufficiently wide to communicate your ideas well. But beyond this, your style should merely reflect who you are. Rarely does one speak as accurately or correctly as one writes. But your style of writing should reflect the style of your speech. Otherwise, it will appear as though someone else wrote your monograph for you, and this always puts a client off—particularly if he was favorably impressed with you at the first meeting.

So be yourself. Don't put on literary airs. Don't camouflage yourself. If you happen to have a flamboyant personality, write flamboyantly. If you are a conservative person, write in a natural conservative style. Don't force your client to deal with a Janus.

Don't puff your proposals or your report. This is extremely common; it reflects our school days, when we were required to write a 2,000-word report and ran out of steam after 500 words. Immediately, redundancy sets in. The same thing is said six times in what we hope will appear to be six different ways. Once is enough. To attempt to mask redundancy and repetition with phrases like "in other words" or "put another way" insults the intelligence of the reader, particularly if you were clear the first time.

Another common method of puffing is lengthily stating in the beginning what the proposal will say and then repeating what the proposal said at the end of the document—thereby writing the same thing three times just to triple the volume of pages. Girth is not worth. You are insulting your client and wasting his time (and yours). Make your point well, but make it once.

Generally, if someone can't express a concept verbally or in writing, he hasn't grasped that concept sufficiently himself. I once had a grade-school teacher who said, "If you can't explain it, you don't know it." A torrent of words doesn't really hide ignorance to a perceptive person. So don't go on and on about something just to impress your client with the fact that you could write that way forever; he won't be impressed—just bored and/or confused. Obfuscation and confusion are what the client is trying to avoid by retaining a consultant. Clarity and precision are called for, and that is what you must offer at the outset.

Make your points as quickly as possible. Make them as succinctly as possible. Be certain that you cover them all. Leave nothing out. A proposal is really a written argument—one you must win! To do so, it is necessary to cover all bases. You must play mental chess by anticipating all opposition and debate; then you must rebut all those points in advance to prevent them from coming up. The client must come away from reading your proposal with no doubts in his mind regarding your efficacy, accuracy and professionalism.

Form

Frank Lloyd Wright hit the bull's eye when he said that form follows function. It does—in writing as well as in architecture. What it is that you are trying to achieve through your proposal will dictate its form. *There is no prescribed form.* Make it good and make it fascinating; your reader will accept any form you choose for it if you do. The business of

    To:
    From:
    Subject:

may be okay, but it can also be trite. Something out of the ordinary is usually expected from a consultant. We expect cliches and jargon from lawyers, bureaucrats, and official memorandum writers—but not from competent, knowledgeable consultants. If a consultant followed the norms, he usually wouldn't be called in the first place.

My own preference is to write proposals like monographs—with accurate, zingy subheads. Then I simply start right in. *I always begin with a covering letter.* The covering letter is really the introduction to the proposal. It is designed as a selling tool in order to make the client *want* to read my proposal.

The Covering Letter

I believe the covering letter is important enough to go into in some detail. It must always be addressed to and written to a particular person. Its form should be that of a regular business letter (on your stationery). If you are on formal terms with the recipient, address him by his surname; if you enjoy a more personal relationship, the salutation should bear his first name. In the latter case, your signature above your full name at the end of the letter should always be your first name only.

Here is an example of a "selling" covering letter:

February 21, 1985

Mr. James Conti, Publisher
Conti & Cameron
124 Front Street
Cleveland, Ohio 41637

Dear Mr. Conti,

Attached is the proposal you requested at our meeting two weeks ago. I'm sure you will agree that it covers all the points we discussed. Additionally, I have come up with a few more ideas to help solve some of your marketing and distribution problems. Some of these were garnered from my files of other clients who had similar difficulties; those problems that reflect your unique situation required innovation and even some daring.

All in all, this proposal represents a comprehensive plan to put Conti & Cameron back on firm ground.

It goes without saying that I would be both pleased and proud to serve your company in the implementation of these plans. (But, I've said it anyhow, haven't I?)

Please let me know your reactions as soon as possible so that I may plan my time accordingly.

Faithfully,

Hubert Bermont
Publishing Consultant

P.S. Attached is a partial list of my clients.
Encl: Proposal
      References

Organization

And what about the proposal itself? Should it be in a completely different style from the covering letter? Not at all. Follow right through. Everything you write must reflect the person you are. Hopefully, however, you are an organized person. *Organization* is what your client needs in his time of strife; he probably came to his dilemma by disorganization creeping into his company. So, first and foremost, your proposal must be extremely well organized. General subjects must be clearly and well titled and identified with Roman numerals or uppercase letters. Subheadings must be equally well titled, accompanied by Arabic numerals or lowercase letters. Each section must fall into its proper sequential place. All of these rules apply to both proposals and reports.

Always use your letterhead for these documents. Further, even though I have been told that it is bad form, I use my letterheads for second and subsequent pages, too. My reasoning is two-fold: first, should any sheet be misplaced, it can be easily identified; second, my letterhead points to me, and this is somewhat of an advertisement.

Format

The most ostentatious, fraudulent puffery is usually found in the graphic format of the proposal. Innumerable executives have complained about this to me by asking, "When will your profession wake up and realize that we are not gullible morons to be taken in by anything and everything purchased at the office-supply store to make a document look fancy?" Post-binders, paste-on gold letters, and even gilded tassels announce that the written material will be in Old English or that between those ornate covers resides an illuminated medieval manuscript.

As to the puffing of the work itself, how would *you* like to receive a ten-page proposal with a title-page, table of contents and three-page index? You must have seen these as often as I.

As Sergeant Friday used to say, "Just the facts, please." Put them on your letterheads, number the pages, and paper-clip them (staples are annoying). Thoreau advised: SIMPLIFY. You would be amazed at how simplification is appreciated in this complicated world of ours. You and I admire it. In truth, so do our clients; they belong to our species.

Also, it's the same now as it was back in school: neatness counts, as does proper spelling. A sloppy paper and/or typographical errors bespeak who you are to the reader. So take time and take care.

The Ineffective Proposal

Let's start with an example of a proposal to the same fictional client whom we addressed in the covering letter. It is a composite of those you and I (and clients) have seen too many of.

> To: James Conti, Publisher
> Conti & Cameron
> From: Hubert Bermont
> Publishing Consultant
> Subject: Marketing and Distribution Proposal
>
> **Objective**
> It shall be the objective of this proposal to describe the various methods by which Conti & Cameron can increase its marketing potential and also increase its distribution efficiency. This proposal will point out a number of ways and means for creating an upward motion on the marketing graph through increased sales.
>
> Furthermore, this proposal will prove that numerous changes in the distribution set-up will decrease operational costs and enhance operational procedure. This enhancement, as will be clearly shown, will manifest itself by means of modern technology, cost control, and the most up-to-date principles of efficiency.

Methodology

I propose that C&C use a methodology to achieve the aforementioned goals by which the following herein set forth would apply

- Maximization of modern marketing techniques.
- Minimization or elimination of outdated marketing techniques.
- Maximization of profits.
- Minimization of losses.

Maximization of Modern Marketing Techniques

The maximization of modern marketing techniques can be accomplished by the creation of book outlets that have never before been approached. The gambling series should be sold in barber shops, casinos, hotels, motels, and every other shop peripheral to gambling sites. Also, there is an entire untapped market for paperback fiction in motels, because many guests find themselves with no source of entertainment except for TV. A plan could be set up where several titles would be available in each room for purchase. Cooking schools have sprung up across the land, but they are not aware of the additional revenue to be derived through cookbook sales.

C&C will not be considered a full-line publisher until it fills out its list with several more categories, that is, mysteries, science fiction, and more self-help books.

Also suggested is a plan whereby dealers receive an additional discount on books they do not return; similarly, C&C representatives should receive an additional commission for every percentage point of drop in their dealer returns. This ratio should be inversely proportionate.

The quantity discounts should be revised as follows:

10 copies or more 40%
25 copies or more 42%
50 copies or more 44%
100 copies or more 45%

Before discontinuing any of the back-list titles that are slow-selling, an attempt should be made to retitle those books along with the appurtenance of new jackets.

Salesmen's input should be utilized more at editorial conferences. This inputting can then be maximized to its fullest extent in editorial decisions.

Minimization or Elimination of Outdated Marketing Techniques
The following techniques and practices should be eliminated immediately:

Full commissions to C&C reps on sales from accounts over six months old.
Automatic rejections on manuscripts that fall into categories not now published by C&C.
Acceptance of returns over six months old.
The current discount schedule.
The lack of communication between the sales and editorial departments.

Maximization of Profits
Maximization of profits will be accomplished in any or all of the following ways:

The full utilization of financial "float" by means of full discounting of bills, investment in CDs of those monies that await payment of invoices bearing no discount, the switching of deliveries from United Parcel to the U.S. Postal Service, the heavier purchasing at greater quantity discounts of supplies as a hedge against inflation, and a time-work study of every employee function.

The Minimization of Losses
The minimization of losses can primarily be accomplished in two ways: The study and extinction of employee theft, and the meticulous verification procedures of all invoices before approval for payment.

Conclusion
This proposal has described the various ways by which C&C can increase its marketing potential and also increase its distribution efficiency. It has also shown how profits can be increased and losses cut.

If all of the aforementioned recommendations are put into practice, there is a chance that C&C will possibly effectuate its goals in the near future.

I feel that I am well qualified to assist and guide C&C in these matters in a consultative capacity. On your request, I would be pleased to quote my fee for this work. You will find that I am hardworking and loyal. All work is done in strict confidence. References will be furnished on request.

Respectfully submitted,

Hubert Bermont
Publishing Consultant

Only a fool would retain me as a result of a proposal like this. Consider all the things I did wrong:

1. I was stiff, formal, verbose, and redundant.
2. I neglected the covering letter.
3. I described for the client in detail exactly how I would tackle every problem. *I gave it all away free of charge!* There is no reason in the world for him to retain me now. He can do it all himself.
4. By offering these detailed recommendations in advance, I have negated my own human fallibility. I would undoubtedly find miscalculations once I waded knee-deep into the project. I have left myself no room for the vital experimentation necessary for successful actualization of the client's goals. Even if I did get this assignment, I would have to account for every one of my errors in my final report. In short, I have painted myself into a corner!
5. I equivocated concerning the efficacy of my solutions by saying that there is a *chance* that C&C will *possibly* effectuate its goals . . ."
6. The heading and subheadings are composed of asinine jargon.
7. This is neither my style of writing nor my style of speaking.
8. I asked for the assignment as though I were submitting a resume for a job.
9. By forcing the client to request a quotation of my fee, I have made one step into two.
10. The proposal was puffed from beginning to end.

This proposal deserves a failing grade. But that was the price we paid back at school. Here in the real working world, the price is far steeper: loss of gainful employment.

While we are on the subject, please eschew submitting résumés or *curricula vita* (which amount to the same thing). Remember that you are not seeking employment in the ordinary sense. Your calling card, a list of your clients, or your brochure is sufficient and will put you onto a peer basis with your prospective client.

The Effective Proposal

An Efficient and Profitable Conti & Cameron Marketing and Distribution Plan

I. CAPTURING A LARGER SHARE OF MARKET The minimal increase in sales volume over the past seven years reflects only the inflationary price increases of the books. This has been deceiving because in actuality the number of books shipped has decreased. This loss of market can and must be turned around by the following means:

1. The penetration of new markets.
2. The broadening of title categories.
3. he infusion of new sales incentives for both sales representatives and dealers.
4. The complete revamping of the discount schedule.
5. The resurrection of some of the backlist nonsellers.
6. The use of sales department experience in the finalization of editorial decisions.

II. EFFICIENT DISTRIBUTION TECHNIQUES It is quite obvious that there have been no changes in the warehousing and distribution methods for the past ten years. New technology and new shipping rates require that systems be modified, altered, and even in some instances replaced.

III. PROFIT INCREASE   The personnel at Conti & Cameron in all of its divisions are competent and work-oriented, but obviously not profit-motivated. A series of incentive plans should be installed to ensure that motivation. No "stick-and-carrot" techniques should be utilized. Carrots alone will do the job. This has been proven successful in a number of my previous assignments.

IV TIME AND PLACE   I propose to implement all of the above recommendations on your site within eight to twelve months. My fee for this is $2400 per month, plus expenses for any out-of-town trips.

Hubert Bermont
Publishing Consultant

Observe what has been accomplished here:

1. I have covered every one of the client's problem areas.
2. I have not repeated myself.
3. I have been brief but comprehensive.
4. I have not promised anything I cannot deliver.
5. I have not told the prospective client *how* I intend to accomplish these things. Remember, *I haven't been retained yet*. I have given him nothing concrete enough to make this a do-it-yourself proposition. If he wants these things done, he must retain me or another consultant.

6. The proposal is an "up" proposal. I leave no doubt that these goals are achievable.
7. The headings and subheading are the answers to the client's prayers. (I know this from our meeting.)
8. I wrote this in my own style (as you can tell from the rest of this book).
9. I asked for the assignment, but I was neither obsequious nor fawning.
10. The six means that I list in Section I are worded in such a way as to make the client understand that I have the particular new markets, title categories, incentives, discounts, etc. at my mental fingertips.
11. By the brevity and lack of detail, I have not locked myself into promises I cannot keep. Concomitantly, I have left myself room for experimentation in the client's behalf while on the project.

Chapter Twelve

The Report

First, let's understand that not all assignments require a final report. In my own practice, only fifty percent have had this requirement. However, I write a final report in one hundred percent of the cases—required or not. This is my requirement of myself. The client always appreciates it. But my reasons are not as altruistic as might appear on the surface. I use the report as a summation of my work, as a piece of advertising, and as a selling tool to cement the client/consultant relationship in hopes that I will be called upon on another occasion—and possibly get referrals.

Just as form follows function, so does the report follow the proposal—in style, content, and format.

The final report is a *progress* report—always. It should cover all the topics brought up in the original proposal, but this time in minute detail. It should highlight the successes and play down (but not hide) the failures. The client now has both documents—proposal and report—side by side in his files or on his desk. Be assured that they will be compared! Not mentioning those goals that were not achieved or those tasks never accomplished will be a glaring oversight in the client's eyes. You may touch on them lightly, but you dare not ignore them.

Here again, the covering letter is equally important. All the same reasons pertain.

Indeed, every rule concerning the proposal is equally valid for the report. To repeat them here would only contradict my own rules about concise writing and redundancy.

The Ineffective Report

The poor report has no covering letter and begins thus:

> To: James Conti, Publisher
> From: Hubert Bermont
> Publishing Consultant
> Subject: Final Report

> **Objective**
> It shall be the objective of this report to communicate the various aspects of work accomplished for C&C over the past eight months, to describe the work not yet completed attended by the reasons therefore, and to render a status objectification of your company as a whole.

> **Work Accomplished**

> 1. As a result of the penetration of various and sundry new markets, sales for the next six months are projected to increase by six percent. This is far short of the goal set, but the following things must be taken into account: I did not have the full cooperation of Mr. Cameron in this matter, thereby causing friction between me and the sales staff; also several new types of retail outlets

could not be convinced that they should display and sell books; we discovered that motel guests stole books instead of buying them; the majority of cooking schools are held in private homes so this market has not as yet been identified.

2. A further study proved that mysteries and science fiction are too risky due to the vast competition in these markets. C&C was correct in not publishing these in the first instance.

3. I am pleased and proud to announce that the additional incentive discount to dealers cut returns by 14 percent.

4. It is too early to determine any effects of the new quantity discount schedule.

5. The backlist titles are now retitled. It is to be hoped that sales for these books will increase.

6. The new policy of not accepting returns over six months old has been announced to our customers. Hopefully they will comply.

7. Mr. Krantz, the controller, is now fully apprised of the means by which we intend to achieve maximization of profits. A report concerning his implementation of these ideas was supposed to be on my desk ten days ago; since I haven't received it, I cannot accurately report progress in this area.

8. As you know, I intended to conduct a time-work study of employee functions. However, union/management negotiations prevented me from doing this.

Conclusion

It has been the objective of this report to communicate the various aspects of work accomplished for C&C over the past eight months and to describe the work not yet done along with reasons for same.

I believe that C&C could well be on its way to an improved status. It is recommended that I be retained for another three months (at the same fee) to complete the work I started; at the end of that time, another report will be forthcoming.

Respectfully submitted,

Hubert Bermont
Publishing Consultant

Undoubtedly you have discovered a goodly number of *faux pas* as you read this report; you probably even winced a few times along the way. But I assure you that this report is average in the aggregate of drivel that spews forth from thousands of copying machines across the country every day.

Let's review in detail everything I have done wrong here, just to be certain that we both recognize all the mistakes.

1. There is no covering letter.
2. Although I properly followed the form of my initial proposal in a general way, I didn't do so in a definitive way. I also left out a number of items that I had promised my client I would deal with (in my proposal). These will be immediately noticed by him.
3. In a petulant, childish, and whining manner, I have informed Mr. Conti that I have obviously run afoul of his partner, Mr. Cameron. Further along, I attempted to knife the controller, Mr. Krantz. Mr. Conti has to live with these people, not with me. I have very deftly slammed the door in my own face.

4. I have written bureaucratese with words and phrases like "maximization," "minimization," "status objectification," etc. All language like this talks down to a client and produces resentment.

5. Although I have been very honest and direct with my client by giving equal weight to my failures and successes, I have ultimately produced a very negative and depressing report. Clients want reassurance from their consultants. Mr. Conti got none from me.

6. The report points up again and again that I was originally merely guessing at the various methods of improvement in my proposal. It is obvious that I hadn't done my homework. My professionalism should be severely questioned.

7. In one area where I proved correct (item #3), I jumped for joy by stating how "pleased and proud" I am—thereby glaringly making this the exception rather than the rule.

8. I rely several times on the future to tell Mr. Conti what the results of my efforts will be, rather than project those results for him now.

9. The report is far too brief, considering the number of tasks I had set for myself in my proposal. This, despite my attempt at puffing by repeating the objective in my conclusion.

10. Under "Work Accomplished" I used paragraph form instead of itemizing (by letter or numeral) the topics discussed.

11. I have made a poor and unethical attempt to set myself up as a crutch for Conti & Cameron by suggesting that they further retain me to complete the work.

In short, unless Mr. Conti is a complete idiot, I have lost a client. I may even have difficulty in collecting part of my fee.

The Effective Report

Again, the covering letter is essential. It performs the same functions as the letter that accompanied the proposal: it serves as an introduction and selling tool for the main document.

November 1, 1985

Mr. James Conti, Publisher
Conti & Cameron
124 Front Street
Cleveland, Ohio 41637

Dear Jim,

Well, the job is done. Attached is my final report. I truly believe—and I'm sure you will agree—that most of our original goals have been actualized.

In addition to this detailed progress report, I have attached specific plans for you to follow to complete those few projects we could not finish within the allotted time.

I found working with your people enjoyable and gratifying. The prevalent cooperative spirit paved my way for a smoother performance. To those I may have missed, please offer my thanks.

Don't hesitate to call upon me at any time if you have any questions or additional problems.

Meantime, please keep in touch to let me know how everything is working out.

Faithfully,

Hubert Bermont
Publishing Consultant

Encl: Progress Report plus attachments

Now to the report itself:

Progress Report for Conti & Cameron

I. SHARE OF MARKET   Already sales volume has increased by six percent. Annually projected, this increase will be minimally twelve percent. To prove that this is not merely a reflection of inflated prices, total number of books shipped has increased 2.6 percent. We have also succeeded (by means of the incentive additional discount) in reducing bookstore returns by fourteen percent. Factoring this in, we have an annual projected sales increase of 18.7 percent at a minimum. With regard to share of market, therefore, the situation has been completely turned around from a negative to a positive one.

Additional Work in Progress to Increase Share of Market

1. Although unable to set up a sales staff meeting with all concerned due to their variegated schedules, I did send a series of memoranda

(copies attached). These described the new
markets to be penetrated and the most logical
approaches to them. Three major casinos are
now displaying our gambling series; the others
should follow, with enough perseverance on our
part.

2. The motel business did not contribute to our
increase. Theft of books by the guests has forced
us to take a different tack. I have sent a memo to
the managers of those motels we are testing
(copy attached). In it, a system is set up whereby
the guests are notified that we hope they enjoy
the book(s), and, in case of non-return, the cover
price will be added to their motel bill. Simple as
that. Watch for good results.

3. The cooking school idea is still "cooking." Since
it was discovered that a majority of these schools
are run in private homes, we have contacted
four mailing list houses so that we may utilize a
mailing piece to reach this market. An outline
for this brochure is attached along with
suggested copy.

4. The new discount schedule is now in effect (copy
attached). Undoubtedly our accounts will
respond favorably.

5. Six old, nonselling works have now been retitled
and rejacketed by the sales staff with the
approval of the respective editors. This is an
interesting reversal of the usual process, as you
know. The results should prove both fascinating
and fruitful.

6. For the first time, the sales staff has taken an
active part in the Spring editorial meeting.
Attached are completed evaluation
questionnaires from every attendee (sales and
editorial). Their positive nature portend well for
C&C.

7. A new incentive sales bonus plan has been devised. A copy is attached.

II. PROFITS Attached is a copy of a fairly lengthy memorandum to Mr. Krantz, your controller. In it I have detailed the following procedures to create a better profit picture.

1. More attention to invoice discount.
2. Investment of monies set aside to eventually pay those bills bearing no discount.
3. The switch from the use of United Parcel to U.S. Postal Service, except where paid for by the bookseller.
4. The heavier purchase of supplies as a hedge against inflation.
5. A completely detailed time-work study procedure (copy attached), which should be put into effect as soon as labor negotiations are over. Also, I have attached a formula for evaluating these results.
6. An investigation of employee theft has thus far uncovered two "silent partners." Unfortunately, one, as you know, was a long-time trusted employee. Statements from these people revealed that minimally $12,000 was stolen during the past twelve months. This amount is comprised of inventory (at cost), supplies, and cash. Formulae set up by top-notch security consultants would indicate that you are losing at least $60,000 annually in this area. This figure should be halved in the next twelve months now that you are aware of the situation and will continue the investigation along the same lines.
7. Our experiment with Mr. Krantz has unearthed $3600 of paid invoices that were either

questionable or unwarranted. A tighter system is
now in force.

Hubert Bermont
Publishing Consultant

cc: Thomas Cameron
   Lloyd Krantz
encl: Memoranda to sales staff, May 15, July 20,
   August 13, 1985.
   Memorandum to motel managers,
   September 23, 1985
   Evaluation questionnaires, Spring Sales/
   Editorial Meeting
   Direct-mail piece outline
   Discount schedule, effective October 1, 1985
   Memorandum to Lloyd Krantz,
   October 3, 1985
   Time-work study procedure plus evaluation
   formulae
   Incentive sales bonus plan

Now consider the careful reasoning behind this report:

1. It follows the initial proposal, which was not
   too detailed in the first place.
2. The title and subtitles followed the goals of the
   proposal, which, in turn, were the goals of the
   client as expressed in the exploratory
   interview.
3. The report is a *progress* report in every sense of
   the word. Following the advice of a very old
   song, it accentuates the *positive* and eliminates
   the negative. It spells S-U-C-C-E-S-S, and gives
   the client encouragement.
4. Wherever work was not completed, it simply
   states so without offering reasons or excuses.

Instead, it supplies the client with the where-
withal to do it on his own. Although these suggestions sound simple, I know (and the client
will ultimately discover) that it will be necessary to retain me again to complete this work.
But I have not built myself in as a crutch to the
client's operation.

5. Mr. Conti is the operating head of the firm. As
   such, he is well aware of any difficulties I en-
   countered with his partner and his controller.
   But nowhere is this mentioned. I have tactfully
   avoided it—to the point of including these two
   obstructive personalities in my thanks to the
   entire staff. This leaves the door at Conti &
   Cameron wide open for me to return.

6. All the successful ingenious devices I hinted at
   in my proposal were described. The failures
   and near-failures were transposed into further
   experiments, which, in turn, were described
   with sincere optimism.

7. The report is written in simple, straightforward language.

8. I have projected results for my client, thereby
   saving him the effort.

9. I have documented everything with copies of
   prior reports and memoranda. This lends
   authenticity to the report. In length, these documents are the bulk of it.

10. I have not once patted myself on the back. The
    report assumes my successes as a matter of
    course. This reinforces my professionalism.

11. I did not hit, bill, and run. My covering letter
    shows my abiding interest by asking the client
    to keep me informed.

Proposals and reports reflect a consultancy. The concepts set forth here naturally reflect mine and those I ad-

mire. They also bespeak the work of consultants who are successful—financially and otherwise.

The world is moving quickly—away from old-fashioned ideas, outdated methods, and trite and archaic language. Precise communication is vital.

Chapter Thirteen

Ethics and Practices

Since consultants are neither organized nor licensed, there is no fixed code of ethics and no set of rules and regulations they must conform to. On one level, each person pretty much adheres to his or her own moral strictures. On this subject, a funny story comes to mind.

A ten-year-old boy was doing his homework while his father sat in the same room, reading the newspaper. The boy looked up and asked, "Dad, what does 'ethics' mean?" The father put down his paper and explained carefully as follows: "Well, you know that sometimes my customers leave things accidentally in the pockets of the clothing they bring into my dry-cleaning store. Suppose, after a customer leaves the shop, I find a ten-dollar bill in one of his pockets. Here is where 'ethics' enters into the situation. The question immediately arises as to whether or not I should tell my partner." It is not for me to tell you how to comport yourself in your newly chosen profession. I can only pass on my own "ten commandments" to which I have conformed without strain over the years, and which may have something to do with the successful relationship I have with my clients.

1. Thou shalt always work to the best of thine ability to ensure the quick success of thy client's project.
2. Thou shalt not waive, lower, or raise thy hourly or daily fee for any one particular client.
3. Thou shalt not become involved in thy client's organizational politics.
4. Thou shalt not accept any fee for personnel placement.
5. Thou shalt not be idle.
6. Thou shalt never "load" time or an expense account.
7. Thou shalt not accept the assignment of any study or investigation that has a foregone conclusion by the client.
8. Thou shalt not lie to a client.
9. Thou shalt not accept a contingency fee.
10. Thou shalt not quit by accepting a full-time position and becoming an employee once again.

How you practice your consultancy will turn out to be a very individual thing according to some of your already ingrained work habits and attitudes. But here is a description of some of my methods, should you find them useful.

Without sacrificing thoroughness, I always work as fast and as soon as possible. Getting an assignment completed quickly frees me to accept other assignments without time conflicts. Juggling four assignments at once sometimes boggles the mind. As a result, my desk is usually cleared when the next call comes through, and I can give the client my undivided attention. (This backfired on me once when a new client noted the neat appearance of my desk. I quoted the old adage "A cluttered desk portrays a cluttered mind." "That's true," he replied. "What worries me is that your desk is empty.") If a piece of work is due six weeks hence, I apply myself to it in such a concentrated way that I generally turn it in three weeks early. I also begin work immediately, even though I may have enough time to start work later, because I like to start when the problem is fresh in my mind. My clientele seem to appreciate this method.

I always come right to the point. Although I am never abrupt when establishing a rapport with a client while attempting to establish his true goals, I am extremely blunt and border on abrasiveness when dealing with the actual problems and tasks at hand. It has always seemed to me that deep down the client appreciates this kind of incisive candor when paying by the hour or day. Friends, relations, or employees of the client may all have their own emotional and/or tangible reasons for telling him what he wants to hear, but my function as consultant is entirely different. For example, I have often told individual clients who have brought me samples of their work with a need for professional evaluation that they have absolutely no talent and that they are wasting their time and money in that particular area; I have recommended that they either give it up or go to school. I can also be just as candid in the opposite case and urge the talented individual on with much more than encouragement. Indeed, I will pick up the phone and immediately put that client in touch with important contacts in the industry.

Another example. An attorney once called to enlist my services. Knowing nothing about my industry, he wanted to invest money in it by opening a place of business and hiring an experienced manager. He was about to sign a long-term lease and wanted my opinion about the location. The site was fifty miles from my office, so it was necessary to book him in advance for a full day's work. I deliberately arrived in my car one hour early so that I could drive around and apprise myself of the territory before we met. The prospects, from every point of view, were dismal. At the appointed time, I told him of my findings in no uncertain terms. It took all of ten minutes. I got back into my car and somewhat abashedly told him that I would have to bill him for my daily fee. His rejoinder was: "Hell, that's the best money I ever spent. You just saved me over $30,000 on a lease that would have been worthless to me. I am grateful." Of course, that was one of my more intelligent clients. Regardless of the client's attributes, I always work the same way.

I draw no line when it comes to blunt advice. I have told the owner of a small business that was suffering from internal theft that his brother-in-law was stealing him blind. I have told the president of a large corporation that his general manager was totally incompetent and was the cause of the loss of a large number of high-calibre junior executives. I have told a client that there ought to be a law against what he was doing. I have told a client that his work was so good that I could guarantee his selling one piece of it for a minimum of $5,000. He did.

About half of my clients don't take my advice. Those that do take only half of the advice. But you will not be paid on the basis of whether or not your advice is taken. You will be paid for advice given. A great number of people make appointments with consultants for strange and even bizarre reasons, most of which they themselves are not aware of. Some of them either have a need for, or will confuse you with, a psychiatrist. They will enter your office, talk freely and constantly for one hour, and leave happily without your having said a word. This is obviously some kind of catharsis for them, and they have no one else they can speak to in a confidential atmosphere. Some clients will use you as a sounding board for their ideas; whether you agree or disagree with them, they act on those ideas anyhow. Some clients want to plunge ahead with high-price, high-risk investment schemes. I always advise testing the plan first, and they ofttimes become annoyed with me. Some clients have a compulsive need to lose large sums of money; I advise them to join Gamblers Anonymous.

Finally, I never take on any assignment that shows every sign of failure and no chance of success. I like winners, not losers.

I wouldn't exactly call these practices techniques. Rather, they are manifestations of who I am. Who you are will dictate your practices and your ethics. After all, you are becoming a consultant to "do your own thing."

Chapter Fourteen

Competition

There is virtually no competition in consulting (with the glaring exception of a majority of government work, which will be discussed fully in chapter 17). Once again, the comparison with the other professions is very close. Each doctor, lawyer, and accountant builds his own clientele. None, to my knowledge, solicit their colleague's clients. After a while, each gains his or her own reputation, which attracts new clients or patients.

There are basically three types of consultants: the independent (you and I), the influence peddler (whom we have discussed earlier in this book), and the large management consulting firm.

In the beginning, I must confess to a certain amount of awe concerning the large consulting firm that is incorporated with a zillion names on the door and letterhead. How could I possibly compete with or stand up to them? Their names are like household words in the business community, and their offices look like banks.

Recall, if you will, those first three calls I received for purely consultative work many years ago. One of them was from a large organization. On my first exploratory visit, the executive in charge opened the meeting by tossing a weighty report across the desk at me. It was eighty pages long and most handsomely (and expensively) bound. The name of the esteemed consulting firm embossed in gold leaf on the cover made me gasp. This was my very first major consulting assignment. Surely no one expected me to stand alongside, let alone be in the same ball park with *them!* I looked up, and the client, his face purple with rage, threw three words at me: "Read that horseshit!" He then went on to tell me that the eminent consulting firm sent in "some young snotnose with a newly minted master's degree in business administration from Harvard" who had no actual experience and nothing to recommend him but an expensive necktie and an attache case that was the talk of the office complex. Three weeks later, the firm presented my client with a bill for $5,000 and the report I held in my hands. This report was a perfect example of a high-school student's attempt to puff up a paper about a book he had never read (as we discussed in a previous chapter). The eighty pages were devoted to defining the problem, complete with a table of contents and index. "Dammit," yelled the client, "I know the problem. I know it well enough to try to get some help around here. I need some solutions." I felt on much firmer ground then.

I offered to tackle the job and complete it in one working week. I went to work on the following day. I was there four hours, when I recognized the impasse. The middle-management executive in charge, who was assigned to assist me in gathering the required data and information, was a total incompetent. He had obviously covered his tracks and fooled my predecessor. He had kept no records in his division for five years, and he had instructed his clerical staff to do likewise. There were no sales records, no packing slips, and no invoices. All that remained were bookkeeping entries in the ledger books in the controller's office. I quickly assessed the cost to management of writing to all its resources requesting duplicate documents and reconstructing the whole picture. At three o'clock, I asked to see my client in private. I explained what I had found, why it would not pay him to put the pieces of the puzzle together, and why I could not give him the answers he wanted. I was careful not to mention the other consulting firm. I strongly recommended that he dismiss his division head for either incompetence or the cover-up of something more serious. I told him that, although I had set the week aside for him, it would not be fair to charge him the full fee, since I could not fulfill my original function. I would put into writing what I had found and simply charge him my daily fee. It was immediately apparent to him, as it had been to me all day long, that the prestigious consulting firm had taken him for a long ride by stretching this futile situation into a three-week project and filing the nonsensical report. One month later, this client called me back and retained me to administer that division on a free-lance basis. I worked on that project for one year and put the division back on its feet.

Since then, I have never worried about competition from the behemoths of the profession—and certainly not from my fellow independents. The bigger they are, the less functional. Small is beautiful. The bigger they are, the higher their overhead and their fees, and the better my chances. Some companies that are highly specialized are effective. But those that claim to be able to solve all problems in all fields under the guise of "management consulting" are pulling the wool over sleeping eyes. Lots of luck to them.

You will have no competition.

Chapter Fifteen

How to Get Clients

When times are good, everyone does well—and consultants are no exception, whether they are old pros or just starting out. But a little-known fact is that when times are bad—recession or depression—consultants (new or experienced) do *better* than most. Why is this so?

Consider that in bad times most businesses are foundering. Whatever smugness the principals enjoyed has long since disappeared. They are painfully aware of the fact that they need help, from any available source. They need help purely and simply to prevent bankruptcy (they may have called you in too late), but your services are urgently needed in bad times.

In an economic recession or depression the headlines scream bankruptcy statistics. At the time of this writing bankruptcies exceed those suffered during the depth of the 1930s' depression; and editorial discussion of this fact is endless. What is seldom heard, however, is that twice as many businesses are starting up than are going under! (Only *bad* news is saleable in this land of ours.) This is because nothing can kill the pioneering, venturesome, entrepreneurial, gambling spirit of citizens who enjoy a free capitalistic society. Now, if anyone needs assistance, it is the person or organization starting up a new venture. And here is the most fertile ground for consultants.

So in the best or worst of times, the consulting profession has the best chances for success. But this is only true if the consultant knows how to take advantage of the opportunities described above, that is, knows how to market his expertise.

Marketing wisdom, as taught in schools and elsewhere, dictates that the market in question must first be identified and then reached. The first part requires research, study, surveys, etc. This can either be purchased or accomplished by the professional in need of identifying his or her market. The second part requires large outlays of time and expense in one form of advertising or another.

Having been a marketing professional of the old school, I had utilized these methods myself in starting up my own initial consultancy. (See Chapter 3.) These along with the usual procedures of making cold calls (as well as lukewarm ones), writing letters, and setting up meetings to acquaint suspects—they were not yet prospects—with my services and, worse, educating them concerning their problems, occupied all of my marketing time.

I am not in any way implying that these tactics didn't work. In fact, as you saw, they did. But I am saying that these accepted methods of starting a practice are long, hard, arduous, and fraught with risk. So another title for this chapter you are reading could well be "If I Knew Then What I Know Now." The accepted method as described above should not be eschewed. It is necessary as an adjunct to your marketing effort. But making it the main thrust allows too much time to ensue before you are making a decent living. It is for this reason that most new consultants are forced to quit and take a position in someone else's table of organization again. The drop-out percentage is higher in consulting than in any other profession.

Applying the "common marketing wisdom," new consultants almost invariably rent a "hot" mailing list, spend untold thousands of dollars on gorgeous, multicolor brochures replete with expensive graphics, and mail them out at enormous postage and handling rates to the prospective firms on that list. The results are invariably nil.

It is at this point that they seek assistance in my office. Having squandered between $5,000 and $15,000 in start-up costs, with virtually no income from consulting fees as yet, they are quite naturally visibly shaken.

They are at a loss to understand why they failed after systematically identifying and reaching their markets. They know that a great number of names on that mailing list need their help badly. Why didn't they respond? Every successful consultant has a brochure; what's wrong with theirs? Would I analyze the brochure copy and tell them where they went wrong?

Now there is nothing wrong with a nice professional brochure. Indeed, it can be quite a selling tool when used properly. (See the chapter on government work.) Proper use precludes sending it out to a bunch of strangers who are not expecting it and who have never heard of you. Put simply, the brochure is to be used on second contact with the prospect and never on the first contact. It is to be left with the client after your first exploratory meeting or mailed to the prospect when he first inquires about your services.

Mailing a brochure cold to a cold mailing list never works because it is analogous to a psychiatrist moving into a new neighborhood, taking names from the phone book and sending out a mailing piece that, in effect, says, "Look, you and I know that you are all in emotional difficulty. I am a trained expert in these matters. Why not give me a call and set up an appointment?" If you received a mailing piece like this, no doubt your reaction would be the same as the reaction you will get from a prospect upon receipt of your cold brochure. It will be relegated to the "circular file," that is, the waste basket.

Your own mailing list from your own Wheeldex or address book is fine. These are people who either know you or have heard of you. But it is rare that this list exceeds one hundred people. When you rent lists of names of strangers in the thousands or tens of thousands, you are flushing money down the toilet. This is also true when you pay dearly for a large advertisement in your trade or professional periodical, describing your expertise and inviting the reader to contact you. Why is this so? Because you are dealing in expertise and advice that requires a client with an immediate and current problem. These problems may be perennial in your industry or profession in that all organizations may experience them at one time or another. But they cannot be perennial or continuous within any one organization for very long, because that organization would cease to exist. In other words, at any given time your market is both narrow and limited. Out of 10,000 organizations, 50 may be experiencing the kinds of problems that you are capable of dealing with at the time that you advertise your services. But you are paying to reach those other 9,950! "I'd be glad to get 10 of those fifty," you say. Of course you would. But what percentage of those fifty saw your ad or took the time to read your mailing piece? A busy executive is looking for information, and he or she automatically ignores advertising in his limited reading time.

"But advertising is a big business, and mailing-list houses have combined revenues totalling billions of dollars every year." Of course they do. But consider:

The most advertising money in all media is spent on reaching the most people who have a constant need for a product or service. Practically everyone drives a car, drinks beer, uses an overnight delivery service, needs a computer, plays computer games, wears shoes, and eats a dry cereal. Everyone also catches cold at one time or another or has a headache. Even if you are only communicating with 50 percent of the population, spending millions to advertise a hemorrhoid medication pays off handsomely.

With regard to mailing lists, it makes all kinds of sense for a publisher of mystery novels, for example, to rent a bona fide list of those people who have at one time or another purchased such a book via mail order. Chances are that his new mysteries will appeal to that mail-order customer now and forever. The same holds true for jewelry, church donations, professional books, etc. Those names are valuable until their bearers are deceased.

However, we in the advice business are not in that kind of ball game. People need doctors and lawyers only at certain times of their lives. Wouldn't doctors and dentists dearly love to know when someone is about to become ill or have a toothache! Wouldn't lawyers love to know when someone gets into legal trouble! (Ambulance-chasers do, but they are not too highly regarded.) It's the same with us. We would all love to know when that consulting project out there is about to be born so that we can pounce on the prospective client with our credentials in hand. We would pay anything for a specially constructed geiger counter that would lead us directly into the offices of the C.E.O.s who are contemplating getting consultative help at the moment.

The answer? It lies in the new and viable marketing wisdom for consultants. We don't reach out to prospective clients. *We have them reach out to us!* The following techniques offered here are well calculated to place you first in the minds of your pre-selected audience.

To repeat, the consultant's market at any given time is both limited and narrow. The market never consists of everyone in a particular field at any one time. The field is already identified; it is your field: chemical engineering, real estate, financial planning, word processing, mainframe computers, publishing, or whatever. The market consists of those in the field who are experiencing problems or need help at a given time. Here is a real-life example of marketing success as it is practiced now:

A major stock brokerage of national repute hired a staff of tax shelter experts. Equipped with this new body of expertise, they were now ready to market it. But who comprised the market? And how were they to be reached? Income level is no indicator, because a family could be earning $150,000 a year and still not have a nickel to shelter. Savings is no indicator because a family could have $250,000 in savings but either not earn enough to shelter and/or have so many tax deductions that the income doesn't require shelter. Yet, the stock brokerage knows that there are at least 50,000 families in any decent-sized community that require tax shelters and don't know how to go about getting them. So they asked those families to identify themselves; they advertised a free seminar in the daily newspaper. It was given at a famous hotel on a weekday evening. I attended that seminar to research the brokerage's marketing technique. Three hundred middleclass and upper-middle-class couples showed up. An impressive array of written material was distributed free of charge at the registration desk. But I had to register to get the material and gain entrance to the seminar—name, address, and phone number.

The seminar was excellent. It consisted of four experts, each lecturing for thirty minutes on his particular aspect of tax-sheltering; oil drilling, limited partnerships, real estate, etc. No hard sales pitch was made. Attendees were invited to stay and speak further with any of the lecturers privately. The following Tuesday morning I received a phone call at my office from the brokerage; and then the sales pitch commenced. They were not calling cold! I had expressed prior interest by attending their seminar. I had identified myself. I had even psychologically obligated myself by attending their free seminar. I could not hang up on them. I had to listen to what they had to say.

Pay careful attention and you will notice that this brand of modern two-step marketing is being practiced everywhere by successful professionals. There are a number of means of accomplishing this two-step process. We shall discuss all of them in turn, starting with the effective one just described.

As a consultant, you usually address an executive with authority fairly high up on the corporate ladder, in many cases the C.E.O. himself. So the longer your seminar, the less likely his time constraints permit him to attend. Your free seminar should never take longer than two hours. It should be held during the working week and the working day. The invitation should be in the form of a robo-typed letter that has the appearance of a *personal* invitation; most word processors are equipped to do this well. You can expect a 5 percent response (attendance) if you address yourself to a particularly vital current problem of your industry or profession.

In most cases, your attendance should not exceed thirty people (600 letters). The attendees must register. Your lecture must be highly informative so that the prospective clients understand how expert you are in your field. All questions must be answered in a forthright manner without holding back.

A number of attendees will approach you after your lecture to exchange calling cards, ask about your fees, attempt to get you to answer problems, attempt to discuss matters outside the parameters of your lecture, and even set up private appointments with you. And these, of course, are part of the pay-offs. Be certain that everyone leaves with your brochure and any other printed material you have that gives testimony to your expertise.

Within two weeks call the attendees personally on the telephone. *Now* they are not strangers. *Now* they will take the call. *Now* you have their attention. Ask whether they found the seminar helpful and whether you may be of further service to them via a no-obligation exploratory personal meeting.

Should you wish to offset your seminar costs or even make a profit on it by charging a goodly fee, OK. But bear in mind that you will cut your attendance considerably and that your original purpose was to have as many people as possible identify themselves as those in need of your consultative advice.

Editors of professional or industrial periodicals in your field are in dire need of the information you have to impart. Here again, you select a current vital problem and discuss it in full—this time in writing. If current enough and cogent enough, your submission will undoubtedly be accepted. Since most publications do not pay for these submissions, they "atone" by fully describing your credentials in the most laudatory terms. Readers will respond, either to you directly or via the publication. This brings clients to you.

How do experts position themselves so that they are quoted by radio and TV commentators as well as by newspaper and magazine reporters and columnists? Do you ever wonder about this? I wondered about it, learned how they did it and became notable, and quotable myself. This brought countless clients to my door.

Let's take an example you are probably familiar with. Up until recently, you could not have heard a financial newscast or have read about the oil industry without almost always hearing or reading a quote from Dan

Lundberg, publisher of *The Lundberg Letter.* If it had to do with crude oil, OPEC or the price of gasoline at the pump, he was quoted. This man had positioned himself as the oil expert; nobody did it for him.

I am proud to say that time and time again I am quoted with regard to the book publishing industry as well as the consulting profession. But it didn't just happen. A "grapevine" is started only when you yourself plant that seed.

Realizing that every good journalist keeps a reference file for any kind of future information he or she may require, a very astute public relations person (who is a friend of mine) developed a singular technique, which was passed on to me. You simply get a list of those journalists and columnists in your field and send them a pressure sensitive label (unpeeled) with your name, address, phone number, and description of your expertise (state-of-the-art of your technology, professional knowledge by subject, etc.). Be certain that the size of your label will fit any size of a Wheeldex or Rolladex. The information is then handy for the journalist at the moment the subject comes up. I send two labels; one for the publishing industry and the other for the consulting profession. It works. I am contacted. I am quoted. The quotes bring clients.

If you are a good speaker, your knowledge and opinions are prized by technical and/or professional associations in your field, provided that you will speak gratis or for a small honorarium. (They will always pay your travel expenses if the meeting or convention is out-of-town.) Solicit these lectures by letting these organizations know that you are available. Waive your fee whenever requested to do so; in return for this, the organization will distribute your brochures and brag about you (their speaker). This also brings clients to you.

One of the best methods of getting clients is by showing off your knowledge via a short, power-packed newsletter, published on an irregular basis and distributed to a highly selective audience of potential clients. Here again it is recommended that the newsletter be sent free of charge. You will find that this constant, beneficent act on your part will get an excellent response to your regular reminder at the end of the publication that your consulting services are available to the reader.

Sometimes the readership eventually comes to rely on this newsletter to such an extent that you may charge heavily for a subscription.

Still another method of getting clients is writing a report. The report is a self-published version of the magazine article we discussed earlier. It is printed and bound professionally and offered either free of charge or for a low price (to cover expenses) by means of space advertising in your trade or professional magazine. It offers the solution or series of solutions to a common, current problem in your field. The back cover describes your consultancy with information about how you can be reached.

The psychology involved here is the same as that employed by the free seminar. These prospective clients with problems have identified themselves to you by ordering your booklet. They have, once again, in effect, raised their hands and said to you, "Here I am." You now have their names and addresses. You may contact them by phone to ask if you can be of any further assistance, you may personally invite them to your seminar, or you may send them your newsletter. They will now listen, because they have introduced themselves to you.

It is commonly accepted in this country that the person who writes a how-to book or manual on any subject is the leading expert in that field. Writing a book about a subject on which you are expert is not as difficult as it seems. After all, you are not producing the great American novel. It is simply a matter of organizing the information you already possess. If you have published articles you need merely arrange them into chapters with connecting text.

These, then, are the successful techniques for getting clients used by today's progressive consultants. Which of them should you use? I recently told my dentist that I didn't have the time to regularly and properly floss my teeth. I loved his answer. "O.K. Then just floss the ones you want to keep." Twisting and paraphrasing his advice: Ignore those methods herein described for those sources from which you don't want clients. But if you want a full client load now, not five years from now, you will do well to apply all of these techniques to your individual consultancy. Because thus positioned in your field, you will have eliminated your competition, you will have eliminated all risk, and you will have guaranteed the success of your professional future.

There is one more thing that will enhance the positioning of your practice and marketing effort. I refer to your *credibility*. Your *credentials*. Recall that when I started I had none, and that is what made it so tough for me that I had to take on my first client free of charge. In those days there was no such thing as The American Consultants League, an interdisciplinary national association I would have joined for additional accreditation. (The American Consultants League, 640 S. Washington Boulevard, Sarasota, FL 34236 (813) 952-9290.) Nor was there The Consultants Institute—the educational division of The American Consultants League—which could have certified me as a CPC, Certified Professional Consultant (same address as the League). Credibility, credentials, accreditation—all from the Latin verb *credere*: to believe. I was long on talent and short on believability. But *you* needn't be.

Chapter Sixteen

Case History

Sometimes in an expository book such as this, it is necessary to concoct a case history that incorporates at least one example of every rule and theory previously set forth. I think we are fortunate, because I truly worked for one particular client on a big project that ideally exemplifies the main themes of almost every chapter thus far in this book. I have only changed the names to preserve the confidentiality that my profession requires. Everything else is written exactly as it happened and nothing is contrived.

To give you the total picture, let's begin at the very beginning. Two weeks after my first assistant came to work for me, she was still trying to sort out and familiarize herself with the many facets of my work. She was further taxed one morning when I announced that on the following day, and for the next two weeks, she would be required to assist me at the annual convention of my trade association. I explained that the association itself was my client and that each year I helped it with its displays and seminars. On the second day of the meeting, I was required to sit on the speakers' dais during the official luncheon. My assistant sat, unescorted, at one of the tables. During lunch, a gentleman on her right struck up a conversation with her. He began in the usual manner at functions like these by asking her about her name-tag. Whom did she work for, what did an assistant to a consultant do, and what kind of work did the consultant himself do? The young lady could only say that she was completely overwhelmed by the industry, by the convention, and by the past two and a half weeks. She said that nothing, as yet, had come together for her, but that the man she worked for seemed to be nice and very competent in his work. This candor obviously struck some kind of chord, because Mr. Bianco presented his card, told her that his firm was about to embark on a huge undertaking, and asked that I telephone him as soon as the convention was over. My assistant could not know then that Mr. Bianco was vice-president of one of the largest companies in the industry.

I wasted no time in calling and setting up an appointment. The meeting lasted two hours, and I did not charge for this exploratory time. I learned that the company was putting up a new building that would cost over 125 million dollars. A very small division would be expanded in this new building. Would I give the architects the benefit of my experience from a commercial point of view concerning this one part of the building? Would I also plan the new budget, the staff, and the inventory, offer innovative ideas, and help the manager of that division adjust smoothly to his new operation? This was a wonderful opportunity for me. I agreed to start work at my hourly fee. Mr. Bianco introduced me to Mr. Packer, the manager of the division in question. Mr. Packer and I went to lunch and hit it off well. I was particularly impressed with his devotion to the company. He had been working there for fifteen years and knew what he was about.

At this juncture let me explain that in any long-term, ongoing project the consultant works the most assiduously and intensely in the very beginning, particularly in a situation of this kind, which calls for simultaneous endeavor

with many different people in many different departments. After the first couple of months, if he has done
well, most of the departments are working synergistically
on his plans and recommendations, the work is carried
on in a more relaxed atmosphere, and his time on the job
is spread out more evenly. So my bill to the client for the
first month was somewhat steep because of the large
chunk of concentrated time I had devoted initially to the
project. With the payment of the bill came a phone call
from Mr. Bianco. He told me that the president wanted
to see me.

Mr. Bianco ushered me into the office and the president greeted me warmly. We had met perfunctorily on
several previous social occasions. He told me that he was
very pleased with my work thus far and that he was certain that, with my help, the project would be a huge success. In fact, he wanted the first year's operation
budgeted at two million dollars. (This was an astounding
sum, considering that the division had done well under
one million in the old building.) "But frankly, Hubert,"
he went on, "your hourly fee is making me nervous because it is open-ended and we don't know how to budget
for it. I would feel much more comfortable with a flat fee
for the entire job." It took me a while to believe what I
had just heard from this multimillionaire whose family
name would soon grace the facade of a new building
costing more than Dulles International Airport. But
maybe, I thought, that was one of his functions as president. I watched my pennies; why shouldn't he? I decided
not to take umbrage. I told him that I could quote a flat
fee, but that he would have to guarantee that the division
would be operational by a given date. He answered that
he couldn't one hundred percent guarantee it, but that
he was fairly certain it would be open by the following
July. On that basis, I demurred, but countered with a
monthly retainer fee. This he accepted gladly, we shook

hands on it, and I received my letter of intent to this effect from Mr. Bianco two days later. The new place became operational *two years* after that, so I had decided correctly in my own behalf. The president, however, had erred because the entire project would have cost him less on an hourly basis, as it turned out.

My first big task, as I saw it, was to figure out how this proposed plant, bursting newborn upon society as it would, could possibly take in two million dollars in its first year. I came up with an entirely new and different merchandising scheme, which I believed to be a foolproof way of attracting the public's attention. It was rejected. They meant to do it in the traditional way. How, I could never glean from them. I was to budget on that basis. Shouldn't we have an alternate, lower budget, just in case? No. I don't have to tell you that they didn't even approach their budget in the first year of operation. Nevertheless, I budgeted their way. It is always the client who has control of a project, not the consultant. This is as it should be.

By this time, Mr. Packer and I had been working closely and consistently together. I was impressed with his knowledge and his experience as well as with the fine relationship he enjoyed with his staff and fellow workers. He paved the way for me in many areas of my work, thereby cutting down on my time and making things smoother all around. The only thing that distressed me about him was that he was having a difficult time adjusting conceptually to the scope of the newly planned operation, which would be triple the size of his former one. For example, to accommodate that much business, it was necessary for me to conservatively budget a payroll of minimally thirty employees. "What will we do with that many people?" he continually asked. In fact thirty would barely be able to handle that much traffic, but he couldn't fathom it.

At the end of one year, my work had come to an end (long before opening day). It merely remained for them to carry out everything that had been planned. As I said before, this took another year, what with labor strikes and other delays. Mr. Bianco called me into his office to thank me for what I had done, and gave me one final assignment. Would I send him a written evaluative report on Mr. Packer's chances of succeeding as manager of this new, larger endeavor, based on my close-hand observation of him for one year? I had mixed feelings about this, to say the least. On the one hand, I felt that I had been retained in part to spy on one of their people, and this was distasteful to me. On the other hand, I felt that this request was only meet and proper for the success of the new division. Since success is always the original and ultimate goal, I filed my report.

I wrote that Mr. Packer was a very valuable employee to the corporation and described in detail all of his fine attributes. I also gave full credit for his assistance to me in my work. I then honestly stated that the new operation seemed to be beyond his managerial ken. I made no recommendations. That was one time when my blunt honesty came hard to me. Mr. Packer was dismissed from their employ, or allowed to resign, as the case may be.

All in all, I enjoyed this project immensely and came away with the gratifying feeling of a job well done. The place is beautiful and functional. I have a tinge of pride whenever I pass it.

Chapter Seventeen

Government Work

"Always remember that the United States Government is the largest purchaser of consulting services in the world. Remember, too, that the United States Government always pays its bills." This is one of the first enticing things a consultant hears when he opens his office. Indeed, it is often this truism that originally lures him to the consulting profession. As of this writing, the federal government spends so much money on outside consultants that it has lost track of the amount; neither the Office of Management and Budget nor the General Accounting Office knows for certain how much it pays out for this service. (They are even hiring consultants to find out for them!) One educated guess is several million dollars per hour.

On the face of it, that's quite an inducement. Any consultant could easily rationalize that:

1. He is a nice guy, so why shouldn't it happen to him?
2. He has been a diligent taxpayer, so why not get some of this money back legitimately?

3. He is finally in a position to make his expertise work for his country.

And all of this is true.

The obverse side of this, however, is rarely discussed.

That side consists of two negative aspects:

1. Recent media investigations have brought to light and confirmed a long-suspected fact: most government consulting contracts (percentage as yet undetermined) are "wired." That is to say that some consultant got there first—whether by friendship, graft, influence, or his extreme competence on a previous assignment. Because most government agencies have policies that require, minimally, three bids when the contract is let for anything over a minimum dollar amount (usually $5,000), those "in" consultants must be put into "competition" with other consultants on any given project. This makes everything "kosher" and in compliance with the Federal Code. It is here that you enter the picture by being invited to bid on that project. In the case of the wired contract, no matter how high your qualifications or how low your bid, you don't stand a chance. If, for example, the project is wired to a man who recently retired from that government agency to set up his own consultancy or to join a large consulting firm, kiss the project goodbye. (This is what is meant by the revolving-door personnel policy.) Of course, these wired bids are neither asterisked nor earmarked for the public in advance. They look like any other legitimate invitation to bid,

so you have no way of knowing. And no one will tip you off, because wiring is shady.

The point is that you will be spending a lot of time for nothing, and time is the consultant's primary investment and inventory.

2. In the case of a legitimate nonwired bid, an inordinate amount of your time will be required. The bureaucracy thrives on paperwork. It is not uncommon for an agency to accompany a twenty-page bidding form with a forty-page booklet explaining how to fill out that form. Intense, endless study is required to wade through this bureaucratese to arrive at an understanding of the rules and requirements. All of this time is spent whether you win or lose the bid. In most cases, the winning consultants never include this prefatory time in their fee estimates. Of course, if they did show it in their publicly disclosed estimates, they would automatically forfeit the project. The government expects and requires this enormous up-front risk investment from all contending consultants. This is your dues.

Despite the saber rattling by each successive administration, wired consulting contracts will persist for the simple reason that there is no way to stop them. Nepotism of one sort or another is a human characteristic; it dates back to ancient Rome and even earlier to biblical times. So let us postpone the discussion of this nefarious practice and deal with the legitimate means of winning a government contract—since there are still thousands of them in the offing every year.

Considering the prodigious amount of red tape (time) the consultant must withstand to properly present his qualifications, the question persists: Is this what you want? The answer, of course, is always a qualified one: Yes, if I can make a profit; no, if I can't. Many consultants who achieve legitimate project awards from the government can and do earn a profit, and many of them do it often; indeed, they find the work quite rewarding. Who are they?

Strangely enough, they come from the two extreme ends of the consulting spectrum. They are either neophytes who cannot and do not consider all the requisite preparation time of value, since they have no other clients anyhow; or they are large consulting firms that specialize in government work and have, over a period of time, acquired a particular expertise more important and significant than that in their original fields, that is, bureaucratic paperwork. They have trained staffs that do nothing else. This is built into the company overhead and is more than amortized by the large volume of government work billed each month.

The vast number of consultants in between those two extremes are far too busy "doing their thing" and sharpening their professional competence to be bothered with red tape and nonsensical administrative procedures. There is one major exception to this, however. The successful, competent professional independent consultant will often accept government work on an hourly, daily, weekly, or monthly basis. This usually deals with a fee below the compulsory bidding minimum. It allows the consultant to work effectively, terminate the project swiftly, leave, submit his bill, and get paid without any hassle. We shall discuss the methods of getting this and other kinds of work later in this chapter.

So the question prevails: Is this work for you? Think carefully before you embark upon this quest, this gamble, this treasure-hunt for the holy grail of the consulting profession—the government contract.

Which Government?

Thus far, we have been discussing the federal government. But by and large, the same principles of avoiding and seeking consulting work apply to other governments as well—state, county, city, and even foreign. Even though our constitution prohibits the federal government from interfering in state and local matters, the latter have notoriously mirrored the federal government in policy and practice. Indeed, the U.S. Government Printing Office has published the "Code for Better Government." Part of its advertised description is ". . . for use as a model for State and local legislation. The goal of this code is to simplify, modernize, and professionalize the purchasing practices of State and local governments." So substitute state, county, or city whenever we talk about government contracts. Beware, however, of the American city today. One after the other are admitting that they are fiscally unsound; their credit ratings for the sale of municipal bonds keep dropping. Further, their mayors are declaring that there seems to be no way out of this catastrophic financial morass. As with private corporations, the first fiscal obligation for a city is its payroll. If there is anything left, the outside consultant may get paid. But many cities are not meeting their payrolls. So be very careful about the city you choose as a client.

Foreign governments necessitate another word of caution. Different cultures have different mind-sets and attitudes. A promise in one country can mean something totally different in another. A contractual clause in one language can mean something totally different in translation. Unless you are totally familiar with the language, social customs, and mores of another country, steer clear of foreign work. Remember, too, the differences in rates of exchange. At this writing, a Canadian contract for $10,000 will net you $8,000 in American money, unless otherwise specified.

The Tool

The government freely admits that it likes to do business with consultants of apparent substance. Your company must exude an image of size and importance. You must also be an "expert." FCAA, the official government acronym for consultants stands for "expert consultant;" the government will deal with no other kind. To insure this for itself, that's what it calls you. The best symbol for all this, says Uncle Sam, is a well-produced, graphically exquisite brochure. In color. Two colors are better than one. Four-color work bespeaks total success. All the government literature on government contracts says so.

The first rule in winning government contracts is to give the government exactly what it wants, or thinks it wants; and it is very explicit with regard to a brochure. This will be your only big financial investment (the others are in time and effort) so be sure that your brochure is professional looking. The way to do this is to retain a fine advertising copywriter and graphics designer. Printers are usually ill-equipped to produce good, original, artistic "make-readies." The government then requests that you brag a lot in your brochure. Tell of your accomplishments in a most immodest tone. If you have staff, give them high billing too. Substance is what they're looking for. But what they call substance, you may call image. You may be the recognized genius in your field, but if you tell them that you work alone out of your apartment, you won't get that $100,000 contract. Do it with pizazz. You won't regret it. Print several thousand of these brochures. The main costs are in the artwork, typesetting, and color, so there is very little difference in price between 500 copies and 1500 copies. As you will see later, you will make very good use of them. Your brochure is your basic introductory tool.

Whenever you contact a government procurement office, you should make available to contracting and technical personnel at the office a copy of your brochure. Be certain that it has lots of illustrative artwork and that it contains the following:

1. Your company name and address.
2. Work now in progress.
3. Major work completed.
4. Type of work for which your company is primarily qualified.
5. Previous government work done, if any.
6. Your name and your qualifications as well as those of your staff, if any. Include education, professional experience, and papers and/or books published.
7. Names and addresses of colleagues whose services are available to your company—particularly those whose qualifications would benefit the project in question. State their curricula vitae.
8. Your security clearance, if you have one. If you are not seeking work with the military, this is not essential.

Unlike private business offices or you, government employees in procurement offices do not regard mailed brochures as junk. Brochures are their stock in trade, so they carefully file and keep them. Your brochure will be around these offices for a long time advertising you. That's why it is so important to make your brochure an outstanding one. It is your best and first foot forward.

The Approaches

There are five methods of seeking government work: personal contact, requests for bidding invitations, negotiation, voluntary unsolicited proposals, and wiring yourself to a contract. We'll deal with them one by one.

1. **Personal Contact.** This method presupposes
   that your base of operations is in or near an area
   in which government offices proliferate. The
   District of Columbia, any state capital, large
   military installations, or any large offices are
   good examples. Government employees are generally friendly, they are somewhat garrulous,
   they love to play up the importance of what they
   are doing, and they cherish the ear that will listen to their tales of woe concerning their work
   overload. For the independent consultant who
   wants to work by the hour, day, or week, it often
   takes nothing more than dropping by to visit
   these people regularly with offers to help with
   the workload—writing reports, doing research,
   writing procedures, writing training manuals, as-
   sisting in training, etc.—to come away with a full
   workload and excellent income. These are not
   bidding situations, and free-lancers are retained
   virtually on the spot. I know of many such people who do this kind of work consistently with no
   advertising or marketing expense and no overhead. Should there be no work for you on any
   particular visit, leave your brochure.
2. **Requesting Bidding Invitations.** The federal
   government buys everything through appropriate purchasing offices. Consulting services are
   no exception. We are talking about the formal-
   ization of the actual bidding and the purchase
   order, as well as the authorization for payment.
   This is so that each department theoretically
   stays within its budget (which it never does).
   When making a purchase, which is originated
   and requested by a particular agency, the purchasing or procurement office sends out invita-

tions for bids. These invitations go only to those
consultants on their bidder's lists. So your first
step, naturally, is to get yourself on those lists.
You would be well advised to contact the
purchasing offices and the agencies simulta-
neously. Again, always enclose your brochure.
The system does not always work in linear fashion, so it is best that purchasing offices and agencies are both constantly aware of you.

Be prepared to receive lots of mail as a result of these efforts. Of all the bidding invitations you receive, you will undoubtedly find that
very few suit you; you will also find a great number for which you are unqualified. (Yes, Virgin-
ia, the government is imperfect.)

Here is another instance of time and effort
the government requires of you. *You must answer
every invitation.* You cannot be passive and remain on the bidder's list. Your response must
indicate in writing that you are unable to bid on
that particular solicitation but wish to remain on
the list. Fail to do this and the government computer will knock you off the bidder's list automatically. This is important, so remember to
respond to each and every invitation. You'll be
kept quite busy.

One more thing. In filling out government
forms, be certain to complete every space,
whether you think it applicable or not. All lowly
clericals and computers spot empty spaces. An
incomplete form does not go through the
channels.

If a bidder's list contains many names, the
purchasing office may send invitations to only
part of each list each time it wants to make a

purchase. However, for the sake of equity, this is done on a rotational basis until each consultant has had an opportunity to bid.

In some instances, the procurement office will want bids from a greater number of consultants than appear on its bidder's list. In these cases, the office will seek bids through advertisements in trade and professional publications, notices in post offices, and other publicized means. The most popular medium is the "Commerce Business Daily," a newspaper in classified format, which is published Monday through Friday by the United States Department of Commerce in cooperation with all government purchasing offices. I strongly urge you to subscribe to this newspaper if you are serious about government work. It contains a wealth of information and is worth its price. (Bear in mind that the government makes no profit on its publications.) You may subscribe for second-class or first-class mail delivery. Even though it costs well over $100, take the first-class route. Some of the invitations bear short notice; by the time you get second-class mail, the bidding may be over.

3. **Negotiation.** Under certain circumstances, which are prescribed by law and applicable regulations, government contracts may be awarded by negotiation with qualified consultants and without formal advertising for bids. For example, a purchase may be made by negotiation if it is not possible to draft adequate specifications or if the project is experimental or developmental.

In purchasing by negotiation, the procurement office makes the routine use of its bidder's list. However, it asks for price

quotations and/or proposals, including detailed
analyses of estimated costs or other evidence of
reasonable prices. These requests for proposals
are sent to a number of consultants so that the
purchase will ultimately be made on a
competitive basis.

   After reviewing the various quotations, the
contracting officer frequently will negotiate with
you further, seeking the most advantageous contract for the government.

4. **Voluntary Unsolicited Proposals.** Any consultant may come up with an innovative concept,
   put it into proposal form, and submit it to the
   government with a request for a contract. It is
   assumed that you are on the cutting edge of the
   state of the art of your particular discipline and
   that your proposal is in fact original.

   In the event that your proposal is favorably
   considered, you should be technically qualified
   to carry through any program that emanates
   from your idea; but the technical merit of your
   proposal will not be based upon your back-up
   facilities.

   Bear in mind that unsolicited proposals are
   more difficult to pass muster because no government funds have been set aside for them.

   There is no specific form required for submitting an unsolicited proposal, thank goodness;
   but here are some of the items you should
   include:

   a. Your name and address.
   b. Number and qualifications of your employ-
      ees, if any.
   c. Description of your facilities, if applicable.
   d. Outline of previous work and experience.

e. Your brochure.
f. Title of proposal and name of principal consultants.
g. A brief abstract of the proposed project.
h. Proposed starting and completion dates.
i. A budget.

Any information contained in a voluntary proposal that is considered to be of a proprietary nature should be clearly identified. A differentiation should be made between proprietary data and patent data when one or both are contained in a proposal. Each of the military agencies has a "Policy Agreement for the Evaluation of Articles of Disclosure." This is a statement of the terms under which voluntary unsolicited proposals are accepted. It should be carefully read and understood by the consultant.

5. **Wiring Yourself to a Project.** Despite my pejoration concerning wired government contracts, it is understood that this practice will continue unabated. Although I do not condone wiring in any way, I would be delinquent in a book like this if I omitted a description of the methods used to achieve this end.

To further dissuade you from attempting what would appear to be sure-fire ways of winning your contract, you should be forewarned that a subsequent investigation could bring you to ruin financially and professionally; you could even be jailed in some instances.

In many cases, wiring seems logical, rational, fair, and even just in the consultant's mind. For example, let us assume that you come up with a brilliant, innovative idea for the government. Let us assume further that you are an acknowledged expert in your field and that you have worked up a comprehensive, cohesive, intelligent plan to implement your brainchild. You submit an unsolicited proposal in two parts. The first part calls for a $4,500 test; the second part, contingent upon the test's success, calls for a $320,000 full implementation of the program. You are immediately given the green light by the agency to proceed with part one, since the dollar amount is below that required for a bidding situation. You make no profit, but you don't mind, because you are eager to test your theories and prove them positive. Additionally, you invest 126 hours of your time without pay. The test is an overwhelming success in every aspect of your original plan. Now comes part two. The $320,000 program will take one year. The budget you submitted with your proposal calls for a profit to you of $46,000 for working on that project during its entirety. The agency is aware of your financial loss in part one. However, you are informed that part two will now go out for bids. A complete description of your program and its implementation, *copied from your original proposal* (which the government bought and paid for) will be incorporated in the invitation to bid. The invitation will be sent to eighteen companies on the agency's bidder's list. Knowing *how* the project is to be done, virtually any company can come in with a lower bid than yours. You lose the project.

Unfair? You betcha. But the agency cannot evaluate your *creative* effort in its budget. It is prohibited by the Code from doing so. Automatically giving you the contract for part two

could start an investigation, you see. Tough. So,
many consultants make deals with agencies beforehand, that is, no part two, no part one. Part
two is now *wired* to part one. The agency has
many ways and means (and mean ways) of seeing
to it that you get both parts. It can open the bid
with such short notice that virtually no outsider
can comply in time; it can word the invitation in
such obscure language that even the pros can't
understand it; it can describe the project in such
a deceptive way that all other bidders will be
forced to quote a higher fee than yours; it can
open the other bids to your eyes so that you have
a chance to change yours after the fact, etc., etc.
All illegal, but all of it being done daily.

Let's take another example. You want to
open the door for yourself to a very important
agency. You feel that if you do, your expertise
can help it for a long time to come and you can
earn a good, steady income. You bid extremely
low on a project—far below cost; you figure that
this is a worthwhile investment. You do the job
in an exemplary fashion. The agency people
love you. You even receive a written commenda-
tion. Considering your expertise, your smooth-
working relationship with the agency staff, and
your results, shouldn't you get the next job automatically? Indeed, wouldn't it be in the ultimate
best interests of the taxpayers if you did? Contemplate the government costs in opening the
bid. You could save them all that. So, once
again, you and the agency people use nefarious
methods to ensure your getting the next
project—and the next one after that.

And what about the fact that you knocked
yourself out for three months campaigning for

your congressman in his most recent election?
Didn't he tell you how grateful he was? And
didn't he tell you that if you ever needed anything all you had to do was ask? Well, don't you
need his good offices now with this bid coming
up?

You get the picture by now. There are as
many ways to wire a bid as there are hands to
manipulate the wires.

One more thing. We have an effective Freedom of Information Act. You may use it to gather evidence and blow the whistle on any agency
that has wired a bid to your competitor. And
you may win your case—but you probably won't
get the job. Agencies don't like to deal with
troublemakers and people who make waves in
general. Nor will you ever hear from many other agencies again. So you have accomplished
nothing.

As Kurt Vonnegut wrote, "And so it goes."

Getting an Edge

There are several ways to gain a competitive edge—and
your competition will usually be enormous, since many
want to feed from this trough.

First, do your homework. In an unwired situation,
the government will rarely play poker with you. Indeed,
as previously stated, it is quite explicit in what it wants,
even though it may use a roundabout way of stating it. In
the private sector, a good consultant will study all the literature available on the other side of the fence, that is,
those books and articles that take the client's part and
teach him how to select a good consultant. Once you
have determined what the client wants in a good consul-

tant, it behooves you to become that for him—provided his needs are reasonable. Well, the government is a client, even though we never hear it referred to that way. Any consultant's customer is a client. And the government has issued guidelines for its executives on how to choose a consultant, what constitutes a good contract, how to purchase services, etc. *Read as many of those documents and books as you can before submitting bids.* Learn the government state of mind. You will be far ahead of that major portion of your competition that doesn't take the time. Here are a few examples of such published documents:

> *Code of Federal Regulations, Title 41, Public Contracts and Property Management*
> *Federal Contract Compliance Manual. Enforcing Rules of Title 41*
> *Armed Services Procurement Regulation Manual for Contract Pricing*
> *Department of Defense Authorization Act*
> *Guide for System Acquisitions*
> *Federal Procurement Regulations*
> *Government Contract Principles*
> *Guide for the Submission of Unsolicited Proposals*
> *Procurement Law*
> *NASA Procurement Regulation*
> *Navy Contracting Directives*

This is only a sampling of what is available at very low prices from the Government Printing Office, but you get the idea. Many publications are on a subscription basis, keeping you up to date as regulations change. Knowledge of how the government makes its purchases of consulting services is not an elective if you want to win contracts. The second way to gain an edge over your competition is by hiring other experts to aid in your quest. This can cost you money, but it puts you into the league of the hardball players. There are a goodly number of experienced, professional proposal writers, for example, who will sell their talents for a fee. They specialize in answering government bidding invitations. Knowing exactly what the government is looking for and what makes it positively disposed toward a particular proposal, these people can be invaluable to you. Their services include everything from giving advice to actually writing the proposal for you to filling out the bid invitation for you, complete with budgets and all pertinent attachments. One such top-notch expert is Herman Holtz. I can recommend him unequivocally as a true professional with integrity. He can be reached at P.O. Box 6067, Silver Spring, Maryland 20906. (301) 460-1506. Don't look askance at this; it isn't the same as cheating at school by having a ringer write your term paper for you. These professional proposal writers are in a legitimate business. After all, if they do help you to get the contract, *you* still have to fulfill all of its requirements.

Preparing Your Bid

You have followed all the steps thus far. You are now receiving invitations to bid from many agencies. You have rejected those that don't appeal to you by writing to those agencies and requesting that you remain on their bidder's lists. You have decided to accept one of the invitations. It is time to prepare your bid.

We shall assume in this case that you didn't retain the services of someone like Herman Holtz, and you decided to it yourself. The first rule in preparing your bid is to do it like the porcupines make love—very carefully. *An invitation to bid is a legally contractual document, and submitting a bid is acceptance of that contract on your part. If you* submit an erroneous bid and you are awarded a contract on the basis of it, the result may be little or no profit to you, or even serious financial loss. A government contracting officer has no authority to revise a contract price to compensate for a mistake on the consultant's part.

So, before preparing your bid, study the invitation carefully and learn exactly what is expected of you. Study every condition and all amendments.

Don't second-guess the government. If you feel that a particular service or step should be substituted in the project, don't do it. Your bid will be declared nonresponsive. Remember what I said before about the government knowing exactly what it wants, right or wrong. There is no use in attempting to delete, change, or modify any clause.

Remember, too, the rule about filling in all spaces on all forms. Here we come to what may be some impasses for you. Government perforce homogenizes everything and everyone. Not to do so would invoke criticism that some things or some people or some groups are getting special unfair consideration. So everyone is reduced to one common denominator. As a result, don't be surprised if your bid invitation looks somewhat like an invitation requesting a bid on 648 L-shaped metal office desks or 23 million standard steel paper clips. Certainly many of the questions you must answer have no bearing on the creative, innovative services and expertise that a consultant offers for sale. You may see questions like:

1. How many local phone calls will this project entail over the next eighteen months?
2. How many long-distance phone calls?
3. How much do you estimate the cost of (1) to be?

4. How much (2)?
5. How many typewriter ribbons do you expect to use on this project?
6. How many miles of travel will be used by the staff during the entire project? What is the cost of this travel?

Once again: you must fill in all the spaces. Stupid questions deserve stupid answers. In this case the agency is demanding stupid answers, since no one could possibly speak intelligently to these issues this early in the game. Just fill in the spaces with anything that comes into your head and the government will be satisfied that your bid is responsive to the invitation. (Bear in mind that they don't know the answers either; they only know what their budget is, and you don't.) But make certain that you will not be holding the bag by underestimating. Now the answers are easy:

1. 3542 local calls.
2. 1821 long-distance calls.
3. $1428.40
4. $4131. 65
6. 126 ribbons.
7. 29,177 miles. $11,854.21

Take Every Precaution

If you have any question about any provision, any clause, or any language in your invitation, take it up with the agency contracting officer before you answer the bid.

If you have any difficulty with the legal language and the agency contracting officer has not answered your questions satisfactorily, you would do well to consult your attorney. In this regard, the government is not determined to trick you or do you in. It's just that the government doesn't know how to put its demands into straightforward, simple language.

So pay particular attention, for example, to the clauses that deal with default, contract changes, and disputes. We shall deal with them somewhat here, but bear in mind that our discussion cannot be exhaustive or even comprehensive, since many agencies have their own variations on some rules.

DEFAULT. A contracting officer may declare a consultant in default of contract even though it was not he but a subcontractor who defaulted. The consultant may be considered in default if he fails to perform any single provision of the contract. The agency may declare the consultant in default if he fails to make sufficient progress at any time during the project to make proper performance likely! When the consultant is in default, the government usually has no obligation to pay him anything, even the amount to cover his costs. Further, the government may let the contract to someone else and charge the original consultant for any excess costs involved in the process! But the most important thing about being in default is that you might concomitantly be in breach—and you can become the defendant in a law suit, and that can wipe you out.

CHANGES. You cannot make changes in the contract, but the agency can. However, the agency contracting officer must make these changes in writing. Otherwise, the purchasing agency will not allow payment on the contract. So, if you are awarded a contract, and if it is subsequently changed, be sure that the changes are signed by the contracting officer and that you approve these changes before you go to work on the project.

DISPUTES. Your contract will read: "Except as otherwise provided in this contract, any dispute concerning a question of fact arising under this contract shall be decided by the contracting officer." This means that you should take up anything questionable in the contract with the contracting officer *before* you sign it and submit it. If your disputes are unresolved, *do not submit your bid!*

All of the above precautionary care applies as well to the proposal on a government purchase to be made by negotiation. In this case, the contracting officer must substantiate the financial stability of the consultant. So you must include your most recent balance sheet and financial statement along with your proposal.

Pricing Your Bid

Up until about fifteen years ago, big steel, the aerospace industry, the shipbuilders, and most other big industry fleeced the government out of hundreds of billions of dollars in "cost overruns." They were able to do this because the government signed contracts allowing contractors to be paid on a cost-plus basis. The "plus" is what ultimately dented the U.S. Treasury. Expenses were inflated and fabricated; the government paid; the contractors danced down the yellow brick road all the way to the banks.

That situation no longer exists. The government now insists that you sign a fixed-fee-expense contract. One complete price for the entire project. The bottom line of your bid must include all labor, materials, overhead, profit, and all expenses. There can be no cost overruns after the fact. The government will not pay for them. This means that, whereas before the government took all the risk, now you, the consultant must take all the risk. Considering inflation and the fact that consulting cannot be planned ahead with anywhere near the accuracy of manufacturing, you stand a good chance of going right down the financial tube.

I could probably write an entire book about how to price a government consulting bid, but it would be foolish, because Howard L. Shenson has already written an excellent one about formulae for fee setting in both the public and private sectors. I recommend it highly. ("The Successful Consultant's Guide to Fee Setting." The Consultant's Library, Glenelg, MD. 1980) In any event, please factor in everything we have discussed in setting your fee, and please be careful.

Submitting Your Bid

If you have come this far, you have run the toughest part of the course. The rest is formality. But with the government, even these formalities are rigid. Inflexibility is most apparent in the rules about submitting your bid on time, that is, before the time fixed for the opening of the bids. Be certain to mail your bid early and then allow for and assume every possible postal catastrophe.

You will not be held responsible for a postal delay if such case is proven, so send your bid certified or registered with a request for a return receipt. This will also exonerate you if a government agency mishandled your bid after receipt.

Be certain that you have adequate postage affixed to your bid. Government purchasing offices will not accept mail on which postage is due. (For God's sake, don't be chintzy at this stage of the game, after all you've been through!)

If you wish to modify or withdraw your bid as submitted, the change or withdrawal must be received by the government office before the opening of the bids.

Again, if you use the mails or telegraph system, be certain to certify or register and get a signature of receipt.

With regard to how many copies to send, where to send them, etc., just follow the directions on the invitation. These are usually stated in simple language.

The Waiting Game

In the nonwired situation, competition is very keen. For the sake of your other clients and your psychological health, you would do well to assume that you will not be awarded the contract. If you are given the award, let it come as a pleasant surprise. One aspect of a good consultant's genius is his acute power of mental projection; he is always three steps ahead in his internalized chess game. So it is common, during this waiting period, for the consultant to proceed with the project cerebrally. This is a total waste of psychic energy. Some egotistical consultants even adjust their calendars by putting prospective clients on "hold." This is utter foolishness. Turn your mind to other things, other projects, your regular consultancy, even to other bids (if you have the bug by now). But forget about the bid you submitted.

Let's be optimists and pretend that you are awarded your contract. (Congratulations!) Unfortunately, like all the foregoing advice, here is another warning. Your bid stated that your contract may at any time be reduced in size or terminated "for the convenience of the government." (By the way, would you have accepted such a contract in the private sector?) If this should happen, the government will settle with you financially for the amount of work you completed. The settlement will be based upon your actual cost figures. Therefore, always maintain accurate, complete financial records that are current during the entire life of your contract.

Best of luck. I hope you are awarded a government contract—if that's what you really want. Only ten percent of all consultants ever seek government work during their entire careers. There must be a reason.

In keeping with the format of this book, it is only fitting that I cite a couple of my own experiences with the government. In neither case did I solicit work or answer a bid. Both times the government contacted me first.

I was once solicited by a very large federal agency to submit a proposal for doing an extensive survey. The young lady who called introduced herself as their new evaluation officer. It seems that the agency had not evaluated the efficacy of its own work since its inception eight years before. (This should be somewhat disconcerting for you at the very least if you pay your taxes at all.) The first meeting took place in my office. She asked for a detailed budget forecasting all of my expenses and my exact profit on the project. This officer told me that the survey was to be in the form of an elaborate questionnaire (which I was to design), that the information required was to come from the realm of higher learning, and that once the contract was awarded in early June, the winning firm would have three months to gather the information, collate it, and write and publish a final analysis of the findings. I immediately told her that a questionnaire would be fruitless because (a) the halls of academe were virtually empty during the summer recess (for this one needs the wisdom of a consultant?) and (b) no one of any substance would give the enormous amount of time gratis to fill out such a questionnaire. This questionnaire would have undoubtedly run twenty pages to give us the statistical information required for meaningful evaluation. The federal "worthy" allowed as how this was all true. I suggested that there were other, more effective methods of getting the information. She asked that I detail my methodology in my proposal. "You want me to do all of this for nothing?" I asked incredulously. "Certainly," she said, "the other nominees are doing it." Well, I thought, maybe I was out of step with the world as far as government work was concerned. Let's give it a go and see what happens. After the official assured me that she was in complete agreement with me regarding the worthlessness of a questionnaire and that any firm that consented to do it that way would of necessity have to fictionalize a final report because of lack of information, I agreed to submit a detailed proposal and budget. I also made her aware of the enormous pressures imposed upon me by her limited time-frame to accomplish the work. She said that it couldn't be helped because that final report was needed by September in order to be incorporated into another larger report that had a steadfast deadline.

Two months past the award date, I heard nothing. I called her. She told me that "the committee" had decided in favor of another firm, but, and these were her very words "Thank you so much for helping us, Mr. Bermont. You know we did need several bids and it was so difficult to find anyone who was qualified to do this specialized kind of work." A wired contract! Well, I used the Freedom of Information Act to find out who got the job and under what conditions. It was awarded to a firm that proposed using a questionnaire. Also, that firm was given two months longer to accomplish the work.

On the other side of the coin, I was called one day by a government executive who asked if I would be willing to go to Denver on a given date, give a four-hour lecture at a seminar of 175 government people, and take on a one-hour question-and answer-period. He agreed to my daily fee plus expenses. I went. I worked. I was paid.

Chapter Eighteen

Consulting Psychology

Whether the consultant admits it publicly or privately, he or she is a libertarian—indeed, almost an anarchist by nature. The very fact that this person has decided to quit the established mode of being gainfully employed, that is, by working for someone else on a full-time basis as an employee, establishes that person as a renegade in our society. The consultant has made the decision some time back never again to be exploited in the business world, and, in an almost Marxist sense, never again to have another profit from his labor directly. (Hopefully, the consultant's expertise will indirectly lead to the client's profit, but that is another matter.)

As further proof of the consultant's libertarian philosophy, expressed or otherwise, he has placed himself in the radical position of marching to the tune of his own drummer—something that most of society is unable to do while employed by others. The consultant has come to terms with his own individuality and decided in no uncertain terms that his inner nature precludes being dictated to by outside forces with regard to his mode of work, his place of work, and his method of practicing his expertise. He has placed himself in the enviable position

149

where no one can infringe on his personal rights, his property, or his person and where no one can exploit him without consent.

This being the case, it now remains for the consultant to succeed in *maintaining* his libertarian views in the world of his clients and his prospective clients. No mean task. But, unless this can be accomplished, success in real terms is not within his grasp. This lofty goal can be reached by means of a set of psychological strategies to be used on himself as well as on his clients. Once learned and practiced to the point where they become habit without strain, the consultant's ultimate success is assured—emotionally as well as financially.

It remains for us to identify these tried and true strategies, and then apply them to our own individual consultancies. This, then, is the purpose of this chapter. It is based on my personal knowledge of many schools of psychiatry, on my own experience as a consultant, and on my sessions with my clients as a consultant's consultant.

The Failure/Success Syndromes

Many consultants languish while complaining about being abused by clients, about unpaid fees, rejected proposals, and all the other ills of the profession. Yet, they do little or nothing to analyze the psychological causes of these failures. Rest assured that the causes *are* psychological—either on the part of the consultant or the client or both. Instead, those consultants who are not realizing their full professional potential usually chalk it all up to "bad luck." Luck is important, but for most consultants, chance circumstances are not the main detriments to success.

The failure syndrome is based on the simple fact that the consultant still fails to accept that he is the cause of his own experience—even though he has left the table of organization to be free of the powerlessness of subordination to someone else's decisions. If you are not succeeding as rapidly as you think you should, you are probably still dealing with the external world—the easy (loser's) way. You are not using your innate courage, daring, self-motivation, and discipline to discover your *internal* world—the more difficult (winner's) way.

Another reason that most consultants fail is that they thereby find themselves in lots of company. As I wrote in my book *How to Compete Successfully in Your Own Field*: Since most people fail, and so few succeed, Freud discovered that failure is much more easily accepted than success. In point of fact, psychiatrists' offices are filled with people who have achieved success in their respective fields and can't handle that success emotionally. Failures usually accept their plight easily.

The consultant's success syndrome is pretty much the obverse of the failure syndrome. Successful consultants, the "lucky" ones, never rely on chance alone. Instead, they are self-determined people who analyze every encounter, good or bad. If the encounter went well, they determine which factors made it so, and they "program" them into their methods of operation for the future. If the encounter did not go well, they do the same thing in reverse, "deprogramming" those factors out of their future dealings with their clients and prospects. In all cases, fearless introspection and objectivity lead them to better psychological tactics the next time, and to fascinating lessons learned. *Introspection* is the key, because it is only the consultant's behavior (your behavior) and reactions that can be changed. *You can never change a client!*

Put another way, successful consulting requires individual sovereignty and the courageous testing of all your individual human possibilities. It requires the daring of thinking about the unthinkable—in this case, all even-

tualities your actions may cause and all your emotions actualized from those eventualities.

All of this takes severe mental discipline and concentration—no less than the concentration required of a
top-notch successful professional athlete. Only the techniques are different, and we shall describe those techniques later in the book.

No one has ever succeeded in any profession without being able to answer the following questions of
himself:

Who am I?
What am I?
Where am I?
Where have I come from?
Where am I going?
Why am I going there?
How am I going to get there?

Simple questions; only the answers are difficult. But
they are far from impossible and do not require years of
psychoanalysis to discover. The answers are already
within you, some manifest and some more covert. They
are more easily come upon by transcription of the questions to:

What kind of a consultant am I?
How good am I?
Where would I like my consultancy to be five years
from now?
How can I get there from here?
Is my current practice comfortable? If not, why not?

The Games Clients Play

The environment of the consultant is the world of clients
and prospective clients. And this environment is not a

friendly one psychologically. Indeed, it is often downright hostile. Hostility is anger unperceived by the person experiencing it and usually by the person receiving it.

Unbeknownst consciously to most clients and prospective clients, they look upon consultants with disfavor. This is so for the following reasons:

1. No one likes to feel helpless in the face of someone else's expertise. We all seem to feel that we should know everything in this "do-it-yourself" society. So the consultant is resented.
2. The principal of any organization feels that his payroll is high enough to expect that his staff should have the expertise to handle all his problems as well as all contingencies.
3. It is commonly known that the consultant's services are required because of his experience, not because of formal training or degrees conferred. Why, then, muses the client, does the consultant have the effrontery to charge fees equal to those of doctors, dentists, psychiatrists, certified public accountants, and lawyers? How dare he?
4. The client feels that the money spent on a consultant could and should be used to train his staff to handle these unruly situations. This would be more of an investment for the future, not a one-time expense.
5. "My God," said one executive vice-president to his staff, after reading a requested proposal from a management consulting firm, "do we now have to hire someone to think for us, too?"

The late Dr. Eric Berne wrote one of the most mutative psychology books of the century. It was called *The Games People Play.* Later, Dr. Thomas Harris, who might be considered a disciple of Dr. Berne, wrote a bestseller called *I'm O.K., You're O.K.* Dr. Harris explained the games people play in the popular terms of "transactional analysis." All of these "games" referred to are hostile ones, engendered by a temporary or permanent aberration of the player. The thrust of both books is that, as aware adults, we needn't play these games with those people. The difficulty lies in recognizing the games —and the hostility behind them—for what they are.

At the time that *I'm O.K., You're O.K.* was released, the publisher, Harper & Row, was my client. I, therefore, had the good fortune to attend the pre-publication sales/editorial meeting at which Dr. Harris, accompanied by his wife, explained his theories to us personally. He did this by enacting small skits with Mrs. Harris thus:

> Dr. H: Dear, where did you hide my cufflinks?
> Mrs. H: I didn't *hide* anything. They're just where you put them, stupid!

Dr. Harris then explained that his query of where Mrs. Harris *hid* his cufflinks was a hostile one—a game he was playing as a manifestation of whatever was bothering him at the time. His wife fell into the trap of playing his game by answering him in kind—hostilely. They then re-ran the skit with Mrs. Harris fully aware and in control of the situation, refusing to play:

> Dr. H: Dear, where did you hide my cufflinks?
> Mrs. H: They are in the top drawer of your bureau, to the right of your socks.

The situation was then reversed in order to show that anyone can become a hostile gameplayer at any time:

> Dr. H: Dear, have you seen my cufflinks?
> Mrs. H: Who do you think I am, your nursemaid?

At this point, Dr. Harris explained that he could have played his wife's game by telling her to take a flying leap, but he preferred not to, since he was aware that something was bothering her that had absolutely nothing to do with the situation at hand or with him. *He refused to take it personally.*

One of my closest friends is a prominent Freudian psychoanalyst in my city. One day several years ago over lunch, he mused aloud that, if his patients listened to and understood an instruction he gave them in the early sessions, they would never need all the years of the heartbreaking pain and expense of the psychoanalytic process. I sat forward and eagerly asked him what that key principle is. *"Don't take it personally,"* he said, "but my patients don't understand the simplicity and truth of this. 'What,' exclaimed a patient just yesterday, 'how can you tell me not to take it personally, when my own mother told me when I was ten years old at the beach to swim out into the ocean and not swim back? How could I *not* take that personally?' I explained that her mother's statement manifested parental abnormality and illness, and that her mother would have said that to any child she had, even if it were Shirley Temple. *That's* what I mean by not taking it personally."

Case History #1

I had just completed a very successful assignment for a client who favored me. His praise was unstinting. He asked me to follow up with another assignment, and requested a price. I told him $4,000. The next day, he telephoned and offered me $2,000. I was furious. My stream of consciousness ran thus: "How dare he treat me that way? His organization is loaded with money—two million dollars for this project alone. He did not quibble with the price of the first assignment ($8,000). He admitted that I had done an excellent job, so he is aware of my credentials and expertise. It would be different if I were a stranger off the street soliciting an assignment. He's got a helluva lot of nerve!" So I told him in an irate voice, "Not only won't I do the job for $2,000; I wouldn't do it for you for $3,995." And I slammed down the receiver—forever closing the door to any further assignments from that organization.

What happened? *I took it personally.* Perhaps this man had just had a dressing down from his comptroller. Perhaps he had just had an argument with his wife. Perhaps he was constipated! Whatever the matter was, he would have treated *any* consultant's fee estimate in a like manner.

Had I learned the lesson of "Don't take it personally," I would have told him that I *could* perform the work for $2,000, since that was his budgetary constraint, but that I would necessarily have to spend less time on the project. He would have accepted this. He would have been grateful for the "favor" I was doing him. I would have been awarded the assignment and kept a client.

Case History #2

My client was the publisher of a prestigious national magazine. I noticed that his manner with me in person and on the phone was extremely quixotic. At times, he was effusive and charming. At times he was downright abusive. It was the latter, of course, that upset me. I used to hang up the phone or leave his office and wonder what I had said or done wrong, unprofessional, or even offensive. But I never came up with anything that remotely made any sense. I analyzed the situation further and discovered a pattern. The man was only abusive in the morning. A few diplomatically placed questions of his staff, and I learned the man was an alcoholic. I know

now, going into a situation, not to take these things personally—especially when I know that I am functioning well and in a thoroughly professional manner.

This kind of hostility comes at you in many different ways. When you have completed the assignment and done your job well, and the client refuses to pay your bill, don't take it personally by heating up a one-on-one argument. He isn't paying *anyone's* bill if he can help it. Turn the matter over for collection in the most *impersonal way*. When the prospective client neglects to inform you that your excellent proposal has been turned down, don't get upset. He didn't inform the other denied consultants either. He's an impolite, inconsiderate bastard—*but not just to you*.

The Games You Shouldn't Play

What are the games that clients and prospective clients actually play? Here are the most common:

GAME #1. O.K., HOTSHOT—HOW GOOD ARE YOU?   For the reasons listed at the beginning of this chapter, prospective clients are continually on the defensive during exploratory interviews with consultants. And this defensiveness usually borders on hostility, resulting from a fear of being "taken." The initial interview, when the prospect has his way, resembles that of a personnel officer interviewing a prospective employee. Most clients have the effrontery to request a resume! And most consultants I know actually offer one!! The words "curriculum vitae" don't camouflage a resume!

Don't play this game. You are a consultant with a particular body of expertise, which is for sale on a freelance basis. You are not looking for full-time employment. But, since we all, at one time or another, have been in the uncomfortable position of applying for a job, the client immediately tries to put us back into that same state of discomfiture in his office.

My own method of responding to a request for a resume, credentials, or any other form of "credibility" is to offer the prospect my client list and suggest that he call those people for references. I don't play his game by offering a laundry list of my accomplishments, hobbies, virtues, and skills. Another method I use is to change the subject right away to "What is the nature of your problem? How can I be of help to you?" I am reminding the client that he is the one with the problem(s) to be solved, not I. My cool, calm, professional voice in asking these two questions bespeaks the fact that I am an expert; no more is to be said on the subject at that meeting. If he wants to tell me about the project at hand, he will have ample time to assess my expertise, experience, and proficiency when he receives my proposal. My credibility will come to the fore in that document.

GAME 2. "I'M THE BOSS."   This game is merely a variation of game #1. It, too, is played out of fear by the client. He wants to assure himself that:

1. he will never lose control of you or of the project,
2. he can ultimately dictate your fee,
3. he and his organization will not ultimately be forced to lean upon you as a crutch, and
4. like an employee, you will always be available to him, no matter what your time constraints or schedule.

Of course, you and I know—and *he* knows—that your time is always your own, to be sold to him in segments of your own choosing; that, as an ethical consultant, you wouldn't fudge the project to keep yourself on board longer than you must; and that ultimate control of any project *always* belongs to the client.

You avoid playing this game by merely stating these facts as a matter of your professional policy.

GAME 3. "WE HAVE NO MONEY." The serious prospective client always has money for an assignment or project. You must learn to distinguish between the prospect, the suspect, and the deadbeat. Poor-mouthing on the part of the client is still another method of attempting to keep your fee down. As a professional consultant, your fee structure is set. You merely let the client know this in no uncertain terms. If he is not budgeted for this particular project, then offer your card, request that he call you when funds are available, and politely leave. Any other kind of discussion in this instance is unprofessional on your part, and the client knows this. In other words, engaging him in this kind of nonsense will cause you to loose your credibility in the client's eyes, so you have nothing to gain and everything to lose by "bargaining."

GAME 4. "I'M A VERY BUSY MAN." This "pulling rank" is still another ploy to put you down. He is no busier than you are. You must politely let him know this. He is conducting a business, and you are conducting a practice. Remember that this interview is still exploratory. No client has ever tried this game once he is paying for the consultant's time; at those prices per hour or day, he's *never* too busy.

When I see a prospective client looking at his watch or taking telephone calls in my presence, I turn the tables. I *never* say, "Well, I see that you are busy, so I won't take up any more of your time." Never. Instead, I tell him that I must leave for a previously appointed consul-

tation (whether true or not). This puts the client properly in his place (and me in mine) without offense.

**GAME 5. "THIS IS ONLY A SMALL PART OF A BIG PROJ-
ECT."** Translated, this means once again, "Keep your
fee down. Whatever you do for us isn't that significant in
the larger scheme of things." Notice now that all of these
games are extremely aggressive behavior on the part of
the client. And all for the same reasons. Perhaps he has
taken an executive assertiveness training course. No matter. His motives are still the same: to put you down and
thereby control the interview as well as the fee. Never
play this game by behaving in an equally assertive manner. It will avail you nothing. On the other hand, you
must never play this game by toadying, either.

Again, you don't play the game at all. Understanding his motives is all you need to win. Your part of the
project is terribly important, or you wouldn't be sitting
in his office. You know it, and the client knows it. You
merely respond by reminding him—even though you
both know that it isn't necessary—of the importance of
every element for the success of the entire project. You
may then tell him of a similar circumstance in which your
expertise facilitated the synergy of the larger whole.

**GAME 6. "I'M A VERY IMPORTANT PERSON IN THIS FIELD,
AND I CAN RECOMMEND YOU TO MY COLLEAGUES."** This
kind of "payment" is supposed to be in lieu of part or all
of your fee. Promises of this kind are not only idle, but
usually mendacious. My experience has been that corporate and organizational clients rarely recommend me to
their competitors, colleagues, and peers. They are very
jealous of the work I have performed for them, and they
don't want anyone else in the field to benefit from it.
Also, despite my ethical standards concerning confidentiality, they fear that I will divulge some part of their

business to someone else. Only clients who are individuals recommend me to other individuals.

So the "carrot" is worthless, and I answer this with: "Of course, I appreciate all referrals, and I'm certain that you will find my work and expertise commensurate with my fee."

GAME 7. "ARE YOU OR YOUR COMPANY BIG ENOUGH TO HANDLE THIS?"   This is yet another ploy to keep your fee down. Little guys should get little fees, is the implication. As an independent consultant with a small staff or no staff at all, you have no business charging Booz Allen fees, is the further inference. Nonsense. The client has done a good deal of investigation before you set foot in his office. Know this, and ignore this game.

GAME 8. "WE'RE IN A BIG HURRY ON THIS PROJECT."   This game is calculated to make you "shoot from the hip" and quote a fee on the spot, in hope that you are in immediate dire need of work. Don't do it. Nine chances out of ten, a bit of investigation or questioning on your part will reveal the fact that the client has been keeping this project on the "back burner" for a very long time. And five will get you ten that it will be months before he awards the project to any consultant and starts up—if he ever starts at all. Take your time. Be understanding about his "time constraints," but insist that you will get back to him in a day or so.

GAME 9. "YOU'VE GOT LOTS OF COMPETITION."   This is a variation of game 8 for the same motives. Don't play. Tell him that you always welcome competition, if true competition it is, considering *your* expertise. Since the client brought up the subject, I force the issue by demanding a discussion of the "competition." No names, of course. But, how many? How long will it take the client to evaluate all of us? Etc. And never, never knock another consultant. You cannot raise your own light by dimming another's.

GAME 10. "WE WOULD WANT YOU TO ASSUME THE FOLLOWING RESPONSIBILITIES."   Absolutely! The more the better. But that should be only one side of the exploratory interview. Consultants don't operate in vacuums. What are the client's responsibilities? Be prepared to list his, and to request that he agree to them in advance. Let him know that consulting is a mutual effort between client and professional. This game is being played by the client to weight the forthcoming agreement or contract in his favor. You would do well to scotch this game early on.

Total Commitment: The Winning Strategy

The attitude of commitment is vital in any endeavor——profession, business, employment, public service, etc. But never more so than in the field of consulting. Indeed, it can safely and unequivocally be stated that commitment to your consultancy is more important—in terms of ultimate success—than your cash reserve, your marketing effort, and even your office itself.

Why is this so? Because a laser-like approach to the building of your practice without diversion or distraction is primal. Because consultants are constantly offered full-time positions by their clients, and it is often necessary to wear "blinders" against these offers. Once these alternatives are even remotely considered, your laser beam will be extinguished, you will float in a sea of indecision, and your practice will suffer from adulteration. This occurs in the same way that a marriage suffers from adultery and a business suffers while a principal is negotiating to sell it. Furthermore, the very *idea* that if your consultancy doesn't pan out you can always try something else, or take a job with so-and-so, dilutes your single-minded effort on behalf of your practice.

Case History #3

A client came to my office to discuss the possibility of becoming a consultant. He is a military retiree, fifty-five years of age, with an impressive amount of expertise in defense electronics. He expressed his problem thus: "Should I take the risk of trying to establish myself as a consultant, or should I accept a full-time position at a goodly salary, which was offered to me last week by a large manufacturer of defense electronics?" My answer was quick and forthright. "Take the job with the manufacturer. You are not cut out to be a consultant. The very fact that it is not anathema to you to be part of a table of organization, after having experienced it for over twenty years in the U.S. Army, indicates that you would be uncomfortable as a free-lancer without a steady income, despite your ample pension. You are obviously not a risk-taker. This is not meant as an insult. True consultants are risk-takers, and they would never even consider your alternative. I have never seen a consultant succeed with one eye on a full-time job."

As we proceed, you will find that psychological strategies are not only played by you with your clients. Some you must play with yourself. This is done by forcing yourself into certain frames of mind, tricks of your own psyche if you will. Consultants are a peculiar breed. They have large egos, they are generally not team players, they are prima donnas in their prospective fields, they feel intellectually superior concerning the basic problems of their industries or professions, and they cannot abide positions of subordination to mediocrity. Although it is undoubtedly true that you could successfully hold down any one of a number of full-time positions in your field by dint of your experience, you must never consider them as an alternative. *You must consider your consultancy a do-or-die proposition.*

Case History #4

An expert named Sally M. became a consultant five years ago, after having been summarily dismissed from a lofty executive position. At that time she vowed she would never work for anyone else again, that she would never again allow anyone to hold total sway over her livelihood, humiliate her, or reject her totally. To ensure these things, she opened a savings account and deposited one-third of all her consulting fees.

She now has enough money for two years of subsistence, even if her practice goes sour with no new clients (highly unlikely). Her goal is to have enough for ten years of subsistence. In this way, she says, no one can tempt her away from her idyllic life-style, no matter how "good" the offer.

Case History #5

Clyde K., an agricultural consultant, was approached by a farm equipment manufacturer to sell the company's wares "on the side" to his clientele for extra income. Clyde accepted.

This consultant lost his objectivity regarding his farmer clients' problems. Those equipment commissions loomed too large in his mind. His expertise became diluted. He lost his credibility with his clients.

Clearly, here was a consultant without sufficient commitment in the first instance. The question of whether he wanted to be a salesman or a consultant should have been resolved long before he became a professional. Doctors, lawyers, dentists, and psychiatrists generally do very well. There are many societal reasons for this. But I believe that the primary reason is that they would never consider for a moment doing anything else. From the day they enter medical school, dental school, or law school, they are *committed* to their professions forever. This makes them single-minded in their careers as well as in their personal lives. But consultants enter their profession as a result of expertise gained rather than degrees earned. If you had spent five years of your life in a Graduate School of Consulting (there are none, except for the home-study course offered by The Consultant's Institute previously mentioned), with the concomitant huge sums of tuition ($40,000-$50,000), you, too, would never consider any alternative to your profession of consulting. Well, if necessary, make believe you did! *Anything* to psyche yourself up to the committed attitude that THIS IS IT!

The Art of Saying No

Consultants who cannot say no to clients, prospects, colleagues, professional associations, family, friends, or salesmen are doomed to failure. Their inability to say no stems from their deep-seated insecurities, and is manifest by a desire to be liked by everyone. This is not to suggest that you become a negative, autistic stinker. Certainly it's nice to be nice—but only when you have the time.

A modicum of self-respect and respect for your practice will prohibit you from allowing deadbeats, time wasters, and wheel spinners from encroaching on your precious time. Aside from your expertise, your time is your primary inventory and stock-in-trade.

Case History #6

Mr. C., a competent financial planning consultant, cannot say no to anyone. Four hours of every day are spent

on the telephone; he allows these calls to ramble on interminably, simply because he cannot bring himself to tell
the people on the other end of the line that he is too busy
to talk to them (something they would respect, by the
way). He accepts every luncheon invitation, whether germane to his practice or not. He answers all two-sentence
inquiries with three- or four-page letters.

As a result, Mr. C. is invariably late for appointments, and his calendar is rife with conflicts. He has attended an assertiveness training course and two time-
management courses, to no avail. He is on the verge of
professional bankruptcy. But everyone "loves" Mr. C.

Case History #7

R. K., a health industry consultant, cannot always be
reached. He feels strongly that certain periods of solitude and being "out of touch" are vital to his personal,
intellectual, and professional well-being. He needs this
time to "still the waters," as he puts it; he needs this time
for clarity, without interruption. During these periods,
no one knows where he is—not even his secretary.
Those clients who know him well and respect his knowledge, accept this somewhat aberrant behavior. Those
who do not know him call him all kinds of names. But R.
K.'s reputation has never suffered. He produces faultless
work, has a full client load, earns over $150,000 per year
in fees, never has a conflict in his schedule, and seems to
have lots of time for whatever project is at hand. (I had
occasion to visit R. K. once. My luncheon appointment
with him was for noon. I arrived at 11:48 A.M. and
breezed past his secretary into his office. He didn't look
up or greet me, even though I stood, smiling foolishly in
front of his desk. At 12N, he looked up and said hello,
adding, "When I say noon, I mean noon, not 11:48. Sorry to have kept you standing there, but I was involved in

a client's flow chart, and I couldn't be interrupted mentally." I had to accept this with equanimity and respect.)

R. K. is known as an eccentric—and he couldn't care less. Mark Twain once said, "It isn't easy to be a *good* eccentric anymore." One way or another, consultants are continually asked for free advice. Respect for your own professionalism demands that you say no just as any doctor or lawyer would. "Here is my card. Just call my office and set up an appointment." Self-respect invariably commands respect from others. No consultant has ever lost an assignment or a client by saying, "I have a client on Thursday morning. How would Friday or Monday afternoon suit you?" You're the doctor; the client is the patient. He has a problem to be solved; you do not.

WHEN THE SUCCESSFUL CONSULTANT SAYS NO:

1. The client asks you to lower your fee.
2. The client asks you to waive your fee.
3. The client asks you to accept the assignment on a contingency basis, that is, if the project goes well you will be paid.
4. The client asks your advice "off the record" at a cocktail party.
5. The client is in dire financial straits.
6. The client offers an assignment based on the fact that your final report will be dictated by him.
7. The client is involved in shady dealings.
8. The client would like a complete and specific methodology of how you can solve his problems—before you are retained officially.
9. The client keeps you waiting interminably in his outer office. Get up, leave your card, and walk out. (If he calls again, ask to be paid for your waiting time.)

10. You are constantly asked to donate your time by a trade or professional organization, after having volunteered all the time you can afford.
11. You are asked for a proposal by a prospective client who has rejected two of your previous proposals.
12. You are invited to dinner on the night before you are to submit a final report.
13. Friends, family, or salesmen drop into your office unannounced.
14. Former clients on the phone (unpaid) for one hour ask, "Do you have time for just one more question?"
15. Colleagues call for a lunch appointment "just to chew the fat." Ask what they want to discuss, and then decide whether it is worth your while to do so.
16. Someone wants to turn a twenty-minute meeting into a lunch or dinner.
17. Someone wants to discuss a business matter "over drinks."
18. The middle-management people of a client organization want to socialize and fraternize.

Case History #8

Paraphrasing an old musical comedy song, H. L. is "just a consultant who can't say no." He has, in the past twelve months alone:

1. taken on more assignments than he can handle —at fees lower than standard,
2. signed contracts with two publishers to write books,
3. offered to accept two speaking engagements —one on each coast—within the same week,

4. signed a partnership agreement with a colleague to do a series of seminars,
5. offered to write a weekly column for a professional magazine, and
6. accepted the position of educational committee chairman of his professional association.

H. L. is now the defendant in two lawsuits and the plaintiff in three others against clients who refuse to pay his bills due to non-feasance.

Consultant's Depression

Consultants are targets for severe emotional depression twice during their careers: when they are starting out as fledglings with too few clients to keep them gainfully employed, and later when they are extremely successful by everyone's standards except their own. I have been subject to both kinds of depression, so perhaps the mental tricks I learned to use on myself to get out of these sloughs will help you, too.

Getting started is difficult. Anyone who says otherwise is either a fool or someone who is trying to sell you something worthless (course, seminar, book, etc.). New clients don't appear fast enough. Referrals don't come when you need them. The practice always grows too slowly to suit you. Try to condition your consciousness to being ever aware of the following basic truths:

1. Those prospective clients out there are neither ignoring you nor rejecting you. To think otherwise can lead to severe paranoia. Actually you are new to the scene and they simply do not know that you exist yet.
2. "Every dog has his day" is no less true for consultants. Doing business at the same old stand in

the same old way for a respectable period of
time inevitably produces clients. Somehow it always "comes together" further down the road.
Always! The trick is to *know* that it will happen
before it does—before you get discouraged and
quit. If you know this and keep it in mind, the
same things will happen to you that happen to all
of my successful colleagues and to me (those of
us who stuck it out).

Every week we get the following kinds of inquiries:

- "I heard you speak two years ago at the annual
  meeting. I'd like to discuss our company's problems with you at your convenience."
- "John Doe sat next to me on a flight to Los Ange-
  les last week. He said you are an expert in the
  marketing of our type of product, and he gave me
  your name."
- "I saw your name in the Yellow Pages."
- "I clipped an article about you last year in our
  trade journal, and I thought I'd contact you."
- "Mary Jones recommended you."
- "I read your monograph, and thought you might
  be able to help us."

And on and on. Most of those "seeds" you are planting
now *will* bear fruit later—if you are still around to har-
vest it. Quit, and all of your planting will have been for
naught. Always bear in mind that, no matter how bleak
things may look now, these good things *will* happen to
you.

Another mental trick I played on myself was this: I
regarded the marketing of my new practice as though it
were a paying client—not soliciting new business *only*
when I had free time, but always setting aside a certain

number of hours each week to make new contacts, no matter how busy I was.

Let us now turn to the depression that besets the successful consultant—one that I still find myself squelching from time to time. Despite the good and plentiful fees, and despite the heavy client load, most consultants constantly deal with the depressing fact that their work is inconsequential. *Rare is the consequential consultant.*

Case History #9

I was retained to set up a completely new marketing approach for a book publishing company—a six-month project. The work completed, I detailed the marketing plan in my final report and submitted my bill. Payment came within ten days, accompanied by a glowing letter of praise for me and my work.

Four months later, I had lunch with the publisher. In the course of the conversation, I asked how the new marketing plan was working. "Oh," he said offhandedly, "we never implemented it. Nothing against your plan, old man, but silly politics with certain members of our board of directors prevented us from going ahead. Everyone at the office is quite grateful to you for your time and work."

Case History #10

A client came to my office to discuss his future consultancy. He had set up a two-hour appointment with me in advance. He travelled 1,800 miles to see me. Upon arriving at my office, he spoke nonstop for the entire two hours. I was able to say virtually nothing. When the time was up, he wrote a check and told me that those were the most profitable two hours he ever spent.

Case History #11

I was retained by the United States Department of the Interior to check the plans of an architect engaged to design a government bookstore. I met with the architect. I then filed a report to my client, U.S.D.I., which stated that the architect's plans were a travesty, totally unworkable, and reflected complete ignorance of book retailing. I was thanked for my report and promptly paid. The bookstore opened, built according to the original plans, producing a daily loss of taxpayer dollars for several years before it was finally torn down.

No matter what your income, work that produces no visible or meaningful consequences can be depressing. Whenever this depression rears its ugly head, I force my consciousness to be aware of the following endemic traits of the consulting profession:

- We are paid for advice given, not advice taken.
- We can only be running streams of expertise. We can force no client to drink from that stream.
- The most difficult concept for a client to accept is change: and change is what the consultant is retained to accomplish.
- Fifty percent of all clients take the advice they pay for. Of that, only 50 percent of the advice is implemented. So consequence can only result from 25 percent of the consultant's total endeavor.

After many hours in front of the mirror, I have finally perfected the Italian shrug.

The Compulsive Consultant

Consultant types are by nature compulsive people. One of the basic reasons for their quitting the table of organization is the need to get on with the job. They cannot abide management telling them all the things that won't work. As independent free-lancers, they are in a better position to get their ideas across, work wherever and whenever they wish, and work as hard as they wish. Consultants are problem-solvers, not problem-makers. Whenever a consultant sees a mess, he or she feels *compelled* to clean it up—immediately. Unfortunately and amazingly, this need is usually greater for the consultant than it is for the client!

All of this is highly laudatory. However, a compulsive person is always prone to impulsive behavior. And that is where the consultant gets himself into trouble.

Because of the need to get on with the job and complete a project as quickly as possible, the consultant impulsively:

1. quotes fees too hastily,
2. starts to work on a project before being officially retained,
3. attends meetings at which he has no business,
4. gives away free advice before his proposal is officially accepted,
5. telephones when he should write, and
6. answers questions from clients when he should be asking them.

Case History #12

I was called to an urgent meeting by the executive vice-president of a large non-profit organization. The urgency was due to the fact that the client was very late in his schedule of publishing a book. At the meeting I was asked whether I could and would a) edit the finished manuscript, b) supervise typesetting, printing, binding, and jacket art, and c) index the book. Also, could I have the entire work completed in five months. (Average time for this is nine months to one year.) I said that I could and would. The vice-president then asked my fee. Eager to get started on the project, I blurted, "$9,000." "Done," he quickly responded, and requested his accounting office to draw a check for half the fee as an advance payment. I was then given two large files pertinent to the project for perusal at my office. The files contained the organization's contract with the author as well as minutes of the meetings concerning the book project. A committee had decided, I learned then, to hire *three* experts for the job: an editor, a book production consultant, and an indexer. That committee obviously had no idea that one person could do it all. As a consequence, the allotted budget was far more than the fee I requested (and which was agreed to so readily and eagerly).

If I had waited one day and gathered the intelligence handed to me, the job could easily have commanded double the fee quoted.

Case History #13

A client for whom I had done a lot of work asked to see me. I arrived at his office at the appointed time. Due to our previous pleasant relationship, the meeting with the client and three members of his staff was quite congenial. The client asked whether I would consider planning and supervising a marketing project. I affirmed that I would. He then asked how I would go about it. I gave him a step-by-step verbal rundown before I realized that his staff was taking down copious notes. The client then turned to his staff members and asked, "Is there any reason why you guys can't do this?" A loaded question from a boss to his subordinates, if I ever heard one. To a man, they shook their heads forcefully. The client stood up, shook my hand, thanked me, and asked that I bill him for the two hours.

As my grade school teacher would have scolded, "Go to the blackboard, and write I'LL GET BACK TO YOU one hundred times." Other people absent-mindedly doodle flowers, stars, or other designs on their notepads. I keep writing, "I'll get back to you. I'll get back to you. I'll get back to you." When the client asks about the fee for a project, say, "I'll get back to you." Go back to your office, weigh all the facts, and think it over carefully.

When the prospective client wants information, say, "I'll get back to you." Mull things over, and decide on the best, most professional way of exacting payment for your expertise.

When the client wants information over the phone, say, "I'll get back to you." Whenever possible, get back to him with a letter rather than a phone call. A letter says everything *you* want said, the way *you* want to say it. Back-and-forth telephone conversation with a client has too much of an urgent, anxious aura about it, and it leads to impulsive talk, which is dangerous to your professional health. As a matter of fact, in any circumstance, a letter is always better than a phone call. Telephone calls have no carbon copies for filing and future verification.

Even when you write, don't mail whatever it is for twenty-four hours. That important letter, proposal, etc. will look different to you tomorrow morning. It always does, after due reflection. Don't be impulsive. Usually nothing is burning, and that extra day to give you a fresh look at the matter can make all the difference in the world. I have a complete file of things that I never mailed but rewrote entirely the following day. A book was published of all the letters that President Truman wrote but never sent.

To make an intelligent decision, you need as much information as you can get. As Andrew P. Garvin wrote in his book *HOW TO WIN WITH INFORMATION: Or Lose Without It*, information makes the difference between a

decision and a guess. (In case history #12, I had guessed
my fee.) The information you need as a working consultant rests with the client. The only way to get that information is by asking the client for it. If he is secretive, he's
a recalcitrant client and worthless to you (as well as to
himself).

Case History #14

A client came to my office with a book project that required professional assistance. The conversation went
like this:

> Me: May I see the manuscript?
>
> He: I didn't bring it.
>
> Me: Do you have one?
>
> He: Yes. I just preferred not to bring it.
>
> Me: You understand, I'm certain, that it is difficult
> for me to address myself intelligently to your
> project without a manuscript in my hand.
>
> He: Yes, but I don't want to show it to anyone just
> yet.
>
> Me: What is the book about?
>
> He: I'd rather not say.
>
> Me: Do you have a working title?
>
> He: Yes, but that would reveal what the book is
> about. I showed him the door.

Case History #15

Conversation in a prospective client's office:

> He: Are you considering any other consultants for
> this project?
>
> Me: Yes, three others.
>
> He: Is your organization properly funded for this
> project?

Me: Yes.

He: Who will be the contact person throughout the project?

Me: I will be the contact person.

He: If and when you decide on the appropriate consultant, when do you want the project to begin?

Me: It is not a case of "if" but "when." We will begin on May 1, at the start of our new fiscal year.

He: And how long do you expect that it will take to complete the project?

Me: No less than four and no more than six months.

He: What do you think the project will entail?

Me: Here is a copy of our plans and projections as well as our goals for the project. Would you like to take the assignment?

He: (After studying the papers he handed to me) Yes.

Me: What would you estimate to be your ball-park fee?

He: I'll get back to you.

I'm learning.

Heading Off Conflict

Life is too short to be lead in "quiet desperation," as Henry David Thoreau described it. Instead, we had hoped to eliminate strife, conflict, anxiety, and frustration when we became independent consultants. Why then is there a steady stream of consultants in my office dealing with the same kinds of fears and anxieties experienced by people without this kind of "independence?" Most of us fail to see grief heading our way, even though the signs are apparent. As stated before, the client environment is generally a hostile one. But hostility has a way of telegraphing itself to anyone on the lookout. Now that you are aware of the hostility, perhaps you will be able to identify some of the warning signals that can only eventuate in a damaging enterprise for you further down the roads of some consultant/client relationships.

Troublesome clients tip you off early, in the same way that poor boxers telegraph their punches. They are late for appointments; they make disparaging remarks about lawyers, doctors, engineers, and other professionals; they haggle over fees; they treat you disrespectfully; they make degrading jokes about the consulting profession ("Did you hear the latest definition of a consultant? One who borrows your watch, tells you what time it is, and bills you for the advice."); they begin sentences with "Frankly" or "In all candor;" they speak conspiratorially about confidential matters that do not and should not concern you; they blame their failures on the work of previous consultants.

Consultants who ignore these tell-tale signs fall into three categories:

1. They are just starting out, and they feel that *any* client is important to the eventual success of their consultancies.
2. They are greedy, and willing to put up with any amount of grief in hopes of eventually collecting a fee.
3. They feel like doctors, who must answer any patient's call, as well as administer treatment under any adverse circumstances for the patient's (client's) own good.

All, of course, are wrong. The first group learns all too soon and well that a) the project will fail, b) the failed project will detract from, rather than add to their professional credibility and c) the time would have been better spent in soliciting a solid client. The second group is wrong, because in most cases the fees are not collected as billed. And the third group is wrong, because the troublesome client never responds to the "treatment" anyhow. The point, however, is the grief suffered by the consultant. Having spotted these danger signals, you should by now have sufficient awareness to quickly determine that you don't need this hassle in your present life—and walk away. This kind of frustration occurred for you in a previous incarnation.

Learn to become a true conscientious objector—by listening with a "third ear," and by paying attention to what you hear.

Further Strategies

Here are some more psychological ploys that work well for consultants:

When confronted by hostility—conscious or unconscious on the part of the client—you will find that the client's "armament" is apparent in his defensiveness. Your *offensiveness*, or attack against his defensiveness, would be futile and damaging to whatever relationship you hope to achieve. It is best to *disarm* the client with a very surprising weapon: the truth. So rare is naked, emperor-wears-no-clothes truth these days that one is always taken aback in hearing it. Throwing up your hands surrender-fashion with remarks to the client such as, "Hey, I came here to help, remember?" or "You must be under an awful lot of pressure to be coming on this way," almost always get the client to drop that defensive position and get on decently with the business at hand. Most consultants prefer to *ignore* hostility; the client is aware of this, and merely pushes harder as a result. Your honestly telling him in some way that you are aware of the negative "vibes" in the room lets the client know that you are forthright and above-board, as well as astute. Put another way, to be guileless is to beguile.

Thoughtfulness is usually repaid in kind; when it isn't, it at least incurs obligation. For example, consultants always do more trade and professional reading than do clients. So read with a scissors and with your clients and prospective clients in mind. Clip and send them articles, notices, etc. with "F.Y.I." and "thought-you'd-be- interested-in-this" notes. You'd be amazed at how well this Chinese water-torture beneficence works for your consultancy. Eventually, they all get back to you with an assignment, a lead, or referral. My advertising copywriter has been doing this "number" on me for years, and in those months that I don't at least recommend him to someone, I feel guilty as hell.

The bestselling book to the contrary, consultants never win through intimidation.

Learn to be aware of your own times of emotional and /or physical stress. Once you have identified them— —from a common cold to a spat with your spouse to floating anxiety about your practice—learn to stay away from your clients during those brief periods. Postpone meetings, be "out" to telephone callers, and don't send out correspondence—until the physical or emotional seige has passed. Work only under the best of conditions.

Do not suffer foolish clients gladly.

Stand up to any aggression and attempt to right any wrong done to you. But do not go beyond to retribution. "Getting even" is a tragic waste of your time and psychic energy, and it will accomplish nothing.

With regard to client confidentiality, try not to receive confidential information that does not concern you or the project at hand. Having this kind of information will engender resentment by the client later, when he discovers that he shouldn't have revealed it to you in the first place. Someone once said, "Two people can keep a secret if one is dead." But someone else once said, "Two people can keep a secret if both are dead."

When you are in a bidding situation, bid outrageously high. Clients do not accept outrageousness as reason for an extremely high fee. Instead, they perceive that you must be the "Cadillac" in your field if you command such a high price, while your competition, bunched together with bids in the same price-range, must be the "Fords" and "Chevys." It works.

Paraphrasing the A.A. creed, have the courage to pursue those assignments where you can succeed, the serenity to forgo those assignments where failure is apparent, and the wisdom to know the difference.

How to Become Your Own Consultant

We have all heard the adage, "Physician, heal thyself." What is being recommended here is, "Consultant, consult with thyself." How come we're so good at solving our clients' problems and not our own? The answer of course, is that we often lose our *objectivity*—our primary consulting asset—when it comes to our own consultancies. Well, it is also said that the surgeon should never operate on his own child, or that the child psychiatrist's child could well be a hellion, even though the therapist's techniques help other people's children. For myself, were I a competent surgeon at the top of my profession, I wouldn't let anyone else operate on my child; and if my child were a hellion, I'd consider myself a failure as a child psychiatrist and as a parent. Our professional problems can and should be laid bare to the same cold objectivity as those of our clients. And we should be our own best consultants. A problem that is unsolvable is a dilemma; and I have yet to meet a consultant in my office who had a dilemma. More often than not, he or she could not find an answer because the wrong question was asked, or because the right question was asked in the wrong way. No more than that—except in those cases where the consultant is psychologically self-destructive and bent on losing.

And why are competent, often talented, bright people asking the wrong questions or the right questions in the wrong way? Consultants are highly intelligent people who are trained to research and solve problems! The answer, of course, is that in the building of their own practices, they have lost their objectivity—that same objectivity that has made them excel in their fields with their clients' projects. (I am risking redundancy here because of the importance of the concept.)

Aspirants to the consulting profession take deep gasps of air and always say (in my office or at my workshops), "This is a B I G step for me." Similarly, practicing consultants are so frightened of losing what they have already gained that they, too, are blocked from thinking things through logically when it comes to their consultancies.

Case History #16

W. R. is a top-notch computer consultant. Having read most of the books in The Consultant's Library and attended numerous seminars, he came to my office, still stymied as to how to market his expertise. I changed the subject momentarily (and deliberately), and told him that we were considering the purchase of an office computer, but didn't know which one would be most suitable for the needs of our publishing division. W. R. proceeded to ask specific questions concerning our operation. After hearing my answers, he smiled knowingly and said, "Your situation is far from complicated. _____ has all the equipment you'll ever need for your tasks. Your program is very simple. The equipment manuals will answer all of your questions. They're written in plain English, so you will have no trouble understanding every step of the procedure. I could make a big deal out of this and charge you for my services, but I came here to get help from you, so why take advantage?" I smiled back, equally knowingly, and said, "Since you have all the information about your so-called problems from our books and the seminars you attended, why can't you use the same logic for yourself that you just used for me? The answers here, too, are simple enough for you to figure out on your own. Our books, too, are written in plain English." "Because," he responded, "there's too much riding for me on my problems, and I can't be objective about them." Well, there was about $8,000 worth of equipment riding on my situation as well as the possibility of fouling up our entire fulfillment procedures; yet, I reminded him, *he* thought that *I* could be objective about *that!* I asked him if he "got the message." He grinned broadly and nodded. "Well," I said, "when you get the message, hang up the phone."

Chapter Nineteen

Full Circle

Soon after the president of my former firm dismissed me (what seems like eons ago), he moved up to an executive position in the owning conglomerate. Not too long after that, I received a telephone call from the executive director of our trade association. He had been requested to find a replacement for that position, and asked me if I wanted to be president of my former company. This director was familiar with my work because the association itself was one of my clients. My answer was, "They couldn't hire me for $50,000 a year (a lot of money in those days). My life is too beautiful." He said that $50,000 a year was exactly what they were offering, since it was what my former boss had earned. He stated further that, although he appreciated my attitude, he regretted my decision. This episode is the kind of stuff that wish-fulfillment dreams and waking fantasies are made of. I extracted every ounce of delight from it. But that wasn't all.

Some time later, my former boss called and invited me to lunch. We hadn't talked since the time he had fired me. Curiosity overcame hostility for the moment, and I accepted the invitation. He was not surprised, after ordering drinks and food (in a lovely restaurant, by the way), that his opening attempts at small talk were falling on deaf ears. So he got to the point. It seems that he had fallen out of grace with the conglomerate, and he was now shoved off into a corner (figuratively and literally) with one secretary and no staff, in charge of the smallest, most insignificant part of the business. His contract was terminating in a few months, and he had been informed by the chairman of the board that it would not be renewed. In other words, he himself had been fired! Recall that I had bemoaned the fact that I had spent ten years with the company before I had been sacked. This man had given thirty-five years of his life to it! It was the only firm he had ever worked for. Still and all, I could not find within myself any compassion for him. Instead, I kept seeing and hearing his fateful last meeting with his superiors in my mind's eye and ear. Undoubtedly he was coldly told something like "You are going nowhere with the company and the company is going nowhere with you." He said that, because he was a shy, retiring sort of person, and because I had become somewhat well-connected in the industry during the past few years as a consultant, he would like to enlist my professional services to help him find a job. I graciously told him that I would see what I could do, but that I would accept no fee, because I was a consultant, not a flesh-peddler. All the while, I mused on his lack of self-awareness. A shy, retiring person doesn't abruptly dismiss an executive after ten years of devoted service and then threaten to withhold his severance pay if he doesn't lie to his staff by telling them that he quit. Nor does a shy, retiring person take this same former executive to lunch thereafter and calmly ask for his help. To the contrary, this man had unmitigated gall—and didn't even realize it.

In a few weeks, I heard of an opening and called him. From an objective point of view, he seemed to be right for the job, and I had never questioned his competence. (Indeed, he had taught me much of what I knew.) He applied, but didn't get the position. Some time later, one of my clients telephoned to ask my advice. It seems that my former boss had applied for a relatively unimportant middle-management position with my client's firm with the full knowledge that the salary was half of what he was currently earning on his job, which was soon terminating. My client was concerned over this state of affairs, and frankly distrustful of the situation. "Will he cut the mustard?" he asked me, since I had worked so closely with the applicant for so many years and knew him so well. I honestly told my client that the risk wasn't all that great. The subject in question was desperate, over fifty years of age, and experienced; he had to make it for his own survival. He was duly hired. He has since been employed by three different companies.

Had I started to write a novel instead of this book, I doubt that I could have plotted it better. They say that truth is stranger than fiction. I don't know. But I'm sure that in this eighteen-year segment of my life, the truth has been more satisfying than fiction.

Partial List of Clients
of Hubert Bermont, Consultant

Acropolis Books, Ltd.
A.F.of L.-C.I.O.
Air Force Association
American Association of
Retired Persons
American Association of
University Women
American Booksellers Association
American Federation of Teachers
American Film Institute
American Forest Institute
Ballantine Books
BFS Psychological Assoc.
B'nai B'rith
R.R. Bowker Company
The Brookings Institution
Catholic University
U.S. Chambers of Commerce
Data Solutions
Electronic Industries
Association
Evelyn Wood Reading
Dynamics
Federation of American Soci-
ety for Experimental Biology
FIND/SVP
Garfinckel's
Goodway
Grossett & Dunlap

Harper & Row
Human Events
Information Clearinghouse
International Reading Association
Journal of Armed Forces
McGraw-Hill
Metromedia
National Academy of Sciences
National Education
Association
National Portrait Gallery
National Recreation &
Park Association
National Rural Electrification
Cooperative Association
National Retired Teachers
Association
National Wildlife Association
Nation's Business
Pitman Publishing Co.
Performance Dynamics
Random House
The New Republic
Retired Officers Association
Smithsonian Institution
Stein & Day, Publishers
U.S. Dept. of Interior
The Viking Press
WETA-TV

Index

189

Recommended Books from
The Consultant's Library

These books, personally chosen by Hubert Bermont, can help you build a thriving professional consultant practice:

The Successful Consultant's Guide to Fee Setting, by Howard Shenson, 72 pages

Top consultants earn $1000 a day and more! Here you'll learn how this is done. Every type of fee arrangement is described, including calculating overhead, billing, quoting a fixed-price contract, incentive contracts, and much more!... $29.00

The Consultant's Money Book, by Michael C. Thomsett. 100 pages

In layman's language, this book shows you how to set up a simple accounting system for your consulting business, including record-keeping, forecasting, financial reporting, budgeting, cash control, and the tax consequences of incorporating.. $29.00

The Consultant's Legal Guide & Forms, by Nancy Pyeatt, Attorney-at-Law. 145 pages

Preventive legal care can save you money and trouble. This book is the consultant's legal bible. Included are: Staying out of court, dealing with clients in a legally correct way, handling litigation, contracts, malpractice, etc. Forms included.. $29.00

The Successful Consultant's Publicity & Public Relations Handbook, by Eugene Hameroff & Sandra Nichols. 80 pages.

Advertising doesn't work for consultants, no matter how much you spend. The key is to get yourself recognized by the media as an expert in your field and to get quoted and mentioned often. All the tricks of the trade are revealed by two highly successful consultants with over 50 years experience between them. $19.00

How to Create and Market a Successful Seminar or Workshop, by Howard L. Shenson. 102 pages.

Shenson is the leading presenter of seminars in this country. Here he gives you the fail-proof formula for making excellent income in seminars and workshops. Included are: Testing the market, getting free advertising, how much to charge, how to sell materials at your presentations, and much more!.. $29.00

The American Consultant's League Annual Directory

An invaluable reference work for those who would like to do subcontracting or who require other consultants to complete bid work. Over 750 consultants listed by field of endeavor. $30.00

The Consultant's U.S. Statistical Guide and Source Finder

This important reference lists: books and periodicals dealing with consulting, billing methods, average fees for each consulting category, computer software for consultants, and more. $39.00

(To order, fill out order form on next page)